THE HOT SEAT

REAL TEENAGE ANSWERS TO LIFE'S REAL(LY) HARD QUESTIONS

BRIAN KULAK

EDUMATCH

CONTENTS

For my students
All of you

INTRODUCTION

It shouldn't have taken a generational pandemic for the world to realize that relationships, in all their iterations, are the foundational and shared period at the end of every educational sentence. While consultants and talking heads profit from the power of a genuine, human relationship, there are countless educators left asking: *What took you so long?*

In fact, the media has always understood how to tap into the good ol' fashioned student-teacher relationship trope. From the 80s classic *Head of the Class* to the 90s smash hit *Boy Meets World*, at the center is the immutable impact a teacher has on the lives of his students. The irony, of course, is that studio execs capitalized on the novelty of such relationships, often painting the teacher as a reluctant hero, scoffed at by colleagues while beloved by a handful of kids whose lives he touched. In this way, these characters represent a caricature of what *could be* rather than a portrait of what *should be*. Of what *is*.

In February of 1999, I returned to my alma mater, Audubon Junior-Senior High School in New Jersey, as the newest member of its English department. I was freshly 22 years old, I taught three grade levels and had four preps, my brother was originally scheduled to be one of my students, and I taught in a corner of the building that can only be described as forgotten, so I don't have to tell you that year one, in particular, was a struggle.

Like all novice teachers, I had relatively no idea what I was doing. No amount of undergrad theory or student teaching experience truly prepares us for the gauntlet that is our own classroom. And that was *before* iPhones, TikTok, and a global pandemic.

I often found myself reading just a chapter or two ahead of my kids in preparation for the next day's class. I slept as if it were a hobby, not a biological imperative. I lived in a perpetual state of self-doubt. I was consumed by earning tenure, thereby working under my own tyrannical set of expectations. I had the dermatological equivalent of a 14-year-old's skin, and I had very, very bad hair.

I had not yet been diagnosed with anxiety.

I had not yet been to therapy.

But like so many educators, I survived year one.

My teaching career was marked by a schizophrenic ebb and flow, highlighted by unshakable connections I made with so many of my kids juxtaposed with a pervasive adult cynicism about what and how I was supposed to teach. Early in my career, I decided, in a predictable *Dead Poets Society* kind of way, that I refused to be an ordinary teacher. If I had to comply with that which was mandated, so be it. But outside of that, I was going to teach my class, my way.

Because education, in its most Puritanical form, too often features a teacher talking *at* his students, expecting compliance over creativity, stressing exams over experience, and preaching grades over growth. Nameless, faceless grown-ups in faraway buildings determine what needs to be taught, and kids are simply the recipients of that content. For me, that just wasn't good enough. No, it didn't take me long to realize I didn't want to be part of the machine; rather, I wanted to disrupt the machine, if not dismantle it. And the only way to do that was *with* the kids.

Eventually, I stopped giving tests.

I rarely wrote kids up.

I rewrote the senior curriculum to reflect the world in which our kids lived.

I brought in novels and short stories that used others' darkness to show kids their own light. At one point, I was responsible for three books, Tom Perrotta's *Joe College*, Joanna Hershon's *Swimming*, and Tawni O'Dell's *Backroads*, being removed from the curriculum at the request of a very small but very loud adult contingent.

I taught *The Perks of Being a Wallflower* as this generation's *The Catcher in the Rye*.

I challenged my kids to compete in a Battle of the Sexes at year's end.

I stopped giving seniors a final and asked, instead, that the kids create a written or video retrospective of their high school lives.

I created a year-long public speaking unit unrelated to the state's curriculum expectations.

I stopped talking at my students.

I started talking with my students.

I started listening.

Because here's the thing: No one asked the kids what they thought.

———

For an English teacher, making connections is implicit to what we do. We ask our kids to make connections to literature, to art, to film, to language, and to each other. However, little of that is possible without connections to us, their teachers. The relationships I am proud to have developed with so many former students is why I make an annual pilgrimage to a Dave Matthews Band concert with dozens of them, why I still play poker with some of them, and why I call so many of them my friends. As I reflect on my time with so many of them, I am reminded that our bond was formed, together, in classrooms C-111 and C-206.

In the Hot Seat.

The following chapters will recall some of the most memorable Hot Seat questions and answers during my 15 years in the classroom. In some cases, those same students reflect on their time in the Hot Seat years later as a means of making sense of who they were as teenagers. Others will share how the experience resonates with them to this day.

Because while the Hot Seat did help some students overcome their fear of public speaking and develop the necessary skills thereof, it was never *really* about that or the grade they received. No, the Hot Seat was about much more than that.

For some, it was a reckoning. For others, it was a rite of passage. For still others, it was an introduction to their world.

For all of them, this is my love letter.

INCEPTION

During that first year of teaching, I made a typical rookie mistake: I underplanned.

My first period, English III (CP) class had just finished its study of John Knowles's *A Separate Peace*, and the following day was a Friday, so I didn't want to start something new only to have to reteach it on Monday. It was then, at the most unassuming time, that a student in the front row, Joe U., known for asking questions ad nauseam, offered, "Why don't we do something like what Ms. Renzi does?"

So, I bit.

"What happens is, Ms. Renzi sits us in the front of the class and says something like 'green,' and we have to talk about it off the top of our heads for a minute or so. She counted it as a test grade—if you did good," explained Joe.

I had to chuckle at both the simplistic genius of the activity and at Joe's adverbial mistake at the end of the sentence. I thought about using the old, "You can't do anything *good*," routine, but I thought better of it. Instead, I made a mental note to teach the good/well lesson later.

We mulled over the idea, and while most of the class groaned incessantly, there were a few soldiers who saw the opportunity for an easy grade and an activity in which they would have to participate once a semester at most. However, I had bigger and better things in mind.

I decided that the questions, or prompts, had room for far bigger possibilities. They had to have some substance, some importance, some life-affirming quality.

So, I brainstormed.

I had to attack this from two perspectives. The first was from my own background and experience, and although I was only 22 at the time, I had the added bonus of a degree in and passion for English. As such, I had been (over)trained to (over)analyze everything I read, watched, heard, and lived. Add a touch of anxiety, and I was well on my way to a deeply introspective platform on which to build this activity.

But, that wasn't enough. If this was truly going to work, I had to flip the script and consider everything I was about to include from my students' perspective. Just because I felt strongly about a particular question and had a grandiose vision for its answer didn't mean the kids would respond the same way. In fact, the premise is no different than trying to project my own love for literature onto my students.

I'll never forget our study of *Lord of The Flies* during which a particularly petulant young man, Liam, asked the question that every English teacher dreads.

"Why does everything have to *mean* something? Maybe this guy just felt like writing a book."

Nevermind that William Golding had created an incredibly prescient, transcendent microcosm of politics and society through the eyes of shipwrecked middle school boys. Nevermind that each boy represents a part of our culture that still exists today. Nevermind that Simon's haunting realization that "Maybe it's only us" could serve as a meme, gif, screenshot, or SoundCloud clip for any number of society's ills, particularly during an election cycle.

Maybe, the man just wanted to write about kids on an island.

Kids don't cross the threshold into each of our classrooms, 180 days a year, and morph into mini versions of us. They bring with them levels upon levels of their own *Lord of the Flies*-esque conflict, drama, insecurity, insight, triumph, and failure. So, much like it would be unfair of me to lecture Liam, and his classmates, about the brilliance of Golding's classic, it would be equally unfair, if not unprofessional, of me to use this new activity as a pulpit rather than as a conduit. What Liam, and scores of students like him, would hopefully come to realize is *everything has meaning*. And like Simon said, "maybe it's only us" who determines such meaning.

The original list of prompts started small. Very small. With no expectation for the number of volunteers, the length of answers, the amount of crosstalk after each response, or my own role in the process, I attempted to tap into universal, if not uncomfortable, themes present in our collective adolescence. Again, having graduated from this school just five years prior, I knew my audience. Additionally, I knew I could help carry a conversation if the need arose. What I didn't know is how reciprocally powerful the Hot Seat would become.

Because of the Hot Seat, my students and I were growing up together, creating more parallel than intersecting lines, and all we had to do to accomplish that was listen to each other. Since then, roughly 1,500 students sat in the Hot Seat and told 1,500 different stories. If the Hot Seat was Audubon's very own Ted Talks, then this book is me sitting in my own Hot Seat, reflecting on a career of human connection.

———

What I am most often asked about is how I came up with the questions. In those early days, most were from my own experience and from a genuine interest in how my students would respond. Sometimes, I would take an idea from something I read, a film I watched, or a conversation I had with a friend. Other times, I would perseverate on a song lyric and turn it into a question. Ultimately, most of the questions were based on what I wished someone would have asked me as a teenager.

Now, as a father of a teenager and an 11-year-old, each question takes on renewed meaning, implied gravity, implicit honesty. In fact, as we sat together at dinner one night, my kids asked if they could "play" the Hot Seat, so we did. Without fail, the questions they chose led them back to their parents' divorce, still only in year one at that time, and how they were processing it. We did have some laughs, and at one point maybe even a little cry, as we answered the questions together and came up with our own.

At the heart of each of our formative years is shared experience. Whether we reflect on that time with a shudder or a smile, consider it a gauntlet or our salad days, we do so as part of a collective. I wrote this book to honor that collective, to thank my students for allowing me to be a part of their lives, and to pay homage to those teachers who inspired me to become one myself.

Now, on the other side of a career deserving of no other adjective than blessed, I realize the Hot Seat isn't as much an activity as it is a philosophy, one that transcends the classroom in which it was created. As a leader, I still use the basic tenets of the Hot Seat every day. With my staff, I have a tendency to ask questions and to seek answers that lean heavily toward the human rather than the practical. With my elementary aged students, conversations around struggle or discipline often start with, "Are you okay?" and end with exactly what that specific child needs. With my friends and family, I committed to a Saturday morning check in, through phone or text, during which I simply asked, "You good?" and let the conversation go where it takes us. And with my own children, I look for opportunities to listen rather than to speak.

Simply put, regardless of the context, if we don't ask, they won't tell. Heck, even if we do ask they sometimes won't tell. But we don't need grandiose questions to start a conversation; we just need the right questions. For the right people. At the right time.

The point is that my list of questions is no more gospel than it is flawed. Perhaps subconsciously skewed toward and away from certain themes, my Hot Seat is only one version. A version that was once mine but became ours. I encourage you to come up with your own lists and use them with people you care about, with people who need to be asked and who need to answer, and, most importantly, with your own kids.

Like any good list, the questions survived several iterations and represent that which provided the most meaningful responses and discussion. As you'll see, many of the questions appear at the end of the chapter to which they best apply. The complete list is safely stowed at the end of the book for your consideration.

Like I said, I started with a minimalist approach. The first ten questions were:

1. *What have you been deprived of so far?*

2. *Describe yourself and your family using only one word for each.*

3. *Are you ready for what lies after graduation?*

4. *Do you think you'll have a better life than your parents?*

5. *Knowing yourself, what is the one thing in life that you know you can't handle?*

6. *Outside of a parent, choose the one person who has helped you become who you are.*

7. *Do you find yourself more anxious or relaxed?*

8. *How would you describe your childhood?*

9. *Do you typically finish what you start?*

10. *When was the last time you cried?*

From there, the list became amorphous. I found myself living my life in search of possible additions to the list. Watching every professional sports team in Philly lose in the finals became a question about failure. Enduring a heart-wrenching breakup from my college girlfriend, whom I was convinced I would someday marry, became several questions about love and loss. Exploring my own childhood, elicited countless questions. Giggling to myself about what always makes me laugh (people falling down) became a question. And on it went. A stream of consciousness. A running commentary. A list of questions that needed to be asked and needed to be answered.

Once I had a veritable list of questions I felt comfortable with, I had to design how the activity would look. Then, I had to name the activity, something catchy and with staying power.

I decided I would keep the general skeleton of what Laura Renzi created, so I put a purposely uncomfortable chair at the front of the room and asked each participant to have a seat. Then, I asked each student to pick a number attached to which was the question. This nuance was particularly important because it created a sense of randomness. I wasn't choosing questions for the kids, the *universe* was. Participants could take as long as they needed to consider the question before responding. For my seniors only, responders could veto their first question and hear a second question before deciding between the two. Once a student started to speak, there was no turning back because the imaginary clock in my head started as did the very real evaluation of the answer.

I always reserved the right to ask follow-up questions, to help a student along with a necessary rephrasing or clarification, or to ask a student to have a seat if the answer went off the rails or had simply run its course. Following that, we would all applaud, a rule I was adamant about, the student would have a seat, I would open up the same question for discussion from the class, and I would often include my own commentary as if I had asked myself the question. For students who clearly could not handle being front and center for the activity, I offered them the option of writing their answer and handing it to me or stopping in before or after lunch to answer to an audience of one.

The grading, as it were, was very subjective, obviously, but also very forgiving. I was asking students to do something they'd never done before, they'd likely never do again, and they'd never do in front of their parents. In fact, in the activity's infancy, I didn't even score based on students' public speaking acumen. That facet of the grading didn't come until much later in the process when I realized how successful and meaningful the activity had become. Ultimately, students often walked away with some sort of A or B in the grade book, but as time wore on, I realized fewer and fewer kids were even asking me "what they got" because the experience had very little, if anything, to do with the score I recorded.

Lastly, as I mentioned, I needed a catchy name for the activity, which was easy to remember and, depending on the kid who would participate on any given day, would evoke some sort of visceral reaction: fear, excitement, agita. I also wanted the name to be generic enough so that it didn't have my fingerprints all over it in the event that it failed miserably. In the end, I did what anyone does when he isn't creative enough to come up with something on his own. I used a cliché.

The Hot Seat.

———

During my initial research for the book, I (ab)used my social media presence, which has allowed me to keep in contact with so many former students. Using a brief Google survey I posted to Instagram, I asked my former students three questions.

1. What was your question?
2. What was your answer?
3. What did you learn about yourself and/or what still resonates with you about your time in the Hot Seat?

Admittedly, I didn't expect students to recall their question and answer with precision, but I knew if they started thinking about their experience in the Hot Seat, something would click.

Over the next several weeks, I had phone calls, DMs, coffee dates, and back-and-forth emails with countless former students. Some remembered their experience right down to what they were wearing that day. Some reminisced about what I said after their answer. Others started our conversation with something like, "I was just talking about the Hot Seat the other day!" Still others shuddered at the thought of the hives that crept up from their chest and onto their necks as they sat in the chair. A few even took the opportunity to consider how they would answer their question now, and for some of those former students, "now" is as a forty-something.

This is the Hot Seat.

2

FAMILY

"What have you learned from your parents?"

It should come as no surprise that teenagers are in a perpetual power struggle with their parents. While navigating their own hormones, pushing boundaries, and coming to terms with being who they are, because of or in spite of their parents, kids answered this question in one of two diametrically opposed ways: they clammed up or they would not stop talking. Both served the same purpose.

The group about which I am writing here was a sophomore honors class with a mix of underachievers, overachievers, and hangers-on. Coincidentally, our school's first-year principal, who doubled as my former basketball coach and unwitting sage, visited during this exchange. So not only did we have what I would argue was the most powerful answer ever provided in the Hot Seat but we also had our very first celebrity guest.

The student in the chair for this question, Emily M., was known for her outspokenness, alternative style, and flair for the dramatic, so when she got this question, she did not disappoint.

"I've learned how not to be a parent," Emily started with very little thought, as if she knew the question were coming. "My father taught me how to run, and my mother taught me how to hide."

Wow, I remember thinking. As was so often the case, I had to make a split-second decision, more often based on the student in the chair than on the question and answer, about whether to open up the conversation or to shut it down. Because I knew Emily was capable, emotionally and intellectually, I challenged her.

"When you say your father taught you how to run, what do you mean?"

"Yeah, I mean things got tough on him so he bolted. What more do you want me to say?"

"I mean do you find yourself running from things? Are you running from this answer?"

"I am definitely not running from this answer! I am not going to tell you that I have learned values or whatever from my parents because I didn't. My dad is a coward and that is what I learned. How not to be a parent."

"Do you have trouble with men in all arenas or just in rela-tionships?" I offered.

"Whattya mean?"

"Well, I mean, do you have trouble learning from male

teachers or have trouble respecting male authority figures—do you have trouble learning from me?"

"No, I mean I hate teachers just like every other kid, but what my mom has taught me is more a general distrust in men and what they tell girls. So I guess I don't hate all men, just men who like me or my mom. I have become very close with my mom over the past couple of years. I think it's based on hatred for my father and men in general."

I could sense the conversation becoming combustible, so I stopped there and tried to get her back.

"Well, thanks Emily, I think you've answered that question as honestly as possible and taught us all something in the process. Sometimes we learn how *not* to act. Sometimes our parents don't teach us the things we see on sitcoms, in films, or even in our own hopeful imaginations. I think that what Emily illustrates is that sometimes, whether we like it or not, we have to search elsewhere for guidance, values, or even a personality. The trouble is in where we look. A teacher? A coach? A friend or his or her family? That process can be just as draining as the realization that our parents stink."

As far as a disclaimer, I felt confident that I had remained diplomatic. Then my principal jumped in with less apprehension than I had expected or would have exercised.

A former special education teacher, head basketball coach and assistant football coach, Don Borden served briefly as the high school's athletic director before taking a job as an elementary school principal about three blocks away. Less than three years later, he was back at the high school as the principal, and he wasted no time acting as Wyatt Earp cleaning up a school that had lost its way. Although we were constantly at odds during my tenure as his point guard, our relationship reached a crescendo, and stayed there when he told me how pleased he was that I was on staff, and I echoed the sentiment.

"I'd like to stop and offer another perspective here. A perspective that may be hard for you to understand, appreciate, or even listen to because I am your principal. Because I am at another station in life, a station as parent, husband, and now provider for two ailing parents, I feel like I have to tell you what I've learned from my parents.

"My parents are both getting older, and frankly, I don't know how much longer they'll be with me. That in itself is enough to make me take inventory and reevaluate what they mean to me. Not a day goes by that I don't remind myself that I will not live in regret once they are gone. Not a day goes by that I don't think about them, appreciate them, and tell them I love them. Now I am not saying I call them every day, and they live in North Carolina, but in some way I reaffirm how I feel about them.

"My feelings for them are all the more important when I consider how my kids feel about me and how I want them to feel about me when we reach this juncture in our family's evolution. I want them to see and feel the same things that I do right now. I will not live in regret when they [his parents] are gone because I refuse to. They have shown me what it means to be compassionate, to cherish family, and to love every day they are with me. That is what I learned from my parents. That is what makes me the man I am today.

"And to give you a further example, at the risk of being long-winded, I have learned what it means to say 'I love you.' I know it is hard for you guys to hear that from a grown man, especially one who is in a position of power. But I have learned that I don't care about that stuff anymore. In fact, I don't just say it to my parents or my family anymore. I would tell you that I have a lot of friends and people who are important to me, not the least of which is sitting across the room."

As the class turned to see my reaction, I stopped to appreciate the gravity of what was being said and by whom. The principal had put himself squarely in the Hot Seat and was receiving an A from the class.

"I would tell Mr. Kulak that I love him and am concerned about what happens to him. I know he is going through a really hard time now [a recent excruciating breakup], and I am genuinely hopeful that it all works out for him. But, I think we have had a relationship that warrants mutual respect and admiration and that is why I would feel comfortable telling him how I feel."

After a brief silence, I felt compelled to share something with the class and with my principal.

"I am reminded of a brief conversation with Mr. Borden prior to my student teaching experience. I saw him at a basketball game, and after we exchanged pleasantries, I told him how terrified I was to student teach to which he simply said, 'Bri, you'll do it just like you've done everything else.' That advice not only got me through student teaching but inspired me to write this book."

Again, the class stopped and this time shifted their attention back toward Mr. Borden. It was a moment that none of us will soon forget: an impromptu game of emotional tennis. At least in small part, the Hot Seat had brought parents and their kids closer together despite the fact that there was only one parent in the room.

————

Class Reunion with Julie W. (Class of 2009):

I was always afraid of the Hot Seat because I like to be prepared (it's the teacher in me). It forced me to learn that being uncomfortable is a natural feeling. I learned to embrace this feeling instead of running from it. I started to get a thrill from not knowing what question I was going to be asked.

My memorable experience in the Hot Seat was when I was asked the question, *"Who means more to you: mom or dad?"* I remember feeling very uncomfortable with having to pick one parent over the other. I have always been a daddy's girl, but at that moment I felt bad for my mom, so I picked them both. I knew my answer wasn't the most honest, and I remember feeling angry with myself for not saying exactly how I felt. From that time on, my first priority on the Hot Seat was to be honest, with myself, and all of my peers who were staring at me. I learned to be comfortable with the uncomfortable feeling that I hated.

It was challenging, fun, and sometimes risky, but I loved it. I learned to be comfortable with the uncomfortable feeling that I hated. I also learned to be honest with myself even if I didn't like the truth. I respected Mr. Kulak for making us do activities like this even though we all dreaded hearing our name being called. I hope some people took this activity and made it their own so it continues to be an effective experience.

Questions about Family:

1. Describe yourself or your family in one word. Explain.
2. How would you describe your childhood?
3. How important are/were grandparents in your life?
4. If your parents split, with whom would you live or how did you come to live with the parent you do?
5. Who means more to you: mom or dad?
6. What do you think your parents were like at your age?
7. Describe what you want your children to be like. Do you want them to be like you?
8. Do you think you'll have a better life than your parents?
9. Do you want your kids to end up following the same path as you?

3

IDENTITY PART I

*"Outside of a parent, choose the one person
who has helped you become who you are."*

O n its surface, this is the kind of question that might seem like a layup for most kids. With a wealth of family, friends, coaches, and mentors from whom to choose, there is rarely a shortage of candidates to help provide the impetus for this response. For some kids, the caveat of not being allowed to select a parent is a blessing because so many of my kids' relationships with their parents were fractured. Some became that way over time and almost exclusively because of poor decisions made by the adults. Some never really had a chance because of, well, poor decisions made by the adults. Still others are simply a product of typical teenage rebellion germane to the collective adolescent experience.

For this question, I offer divergent responses from two completely different high school seniors: Alexis Y. and Megan M.

Alexis came to my class with a pronounced chip on her shoulder, the kind that she could remove or replace at a moment's notice. To be fair, that chip's angst and anger were never directed toward me, or any other teacher as far as I could tell, but, rather, toward the people with whom she chose to surround herself. Perpetually pony-tailed, Lex would typically wear basketball shorts, an oversized t-shirt, and her signature glasses to school and then, from what I can tell, wear it all again at night. Not only was she the antithesis of a "girly girl," but she quite literally wore her sexuality with pride. Still, more often than not, Lex came to class with a chewed-up pen in between a kind smile, took her seat with her back against the radiator at the far side of the room, and actively participated.

I liked Alexis before she took the Hot Seat.

I respected her when she was finished.

"I wish my mother was never an alcoholic, my mom and dad had never gotten divorced, and also wish I had a stable home," she started.

From the jump, she didn't really answer the question and was taking it in her own direction. The "I wish" at the beginning of her response took it from practical to theoretical, but I wasn't about to interrupt a kid willing to share with this level of honesty.

"My mom's dad was an alcoholic and he passed away from Cirrhosis. When that happened, my mom became an alcoholic.

She lost herself in it, so she self-medicates. She has no job, no money, no car, nothing. Her kids don't live with her; my dad didn't want to put up with that, and he was paying all the bills with no help.

"As a little kid, I had to fend for myself and make my way through life. And my famous quote is 'you never know how strong you are until being strong is the only choice you have left'."

Lex admitted to having that quote tattooed on her ribs to remind her of how far she had come. She also said that she had been on her own since she was 13. Back then, she lived with a friend, who later became her girlfriend, during high school. At the time of her answer, she was an adult with a full-time job at a car dealership, and she had shared that she had to sort of "househop" until she could make enough money to move out on her own.

I had a feeling where this was going, and I knew she wouldn't come out and say that the person who had the most significant influence on her was *herself*. The answer continued down this say-it-without-saying-it path, and most of the people in the room, including me, knew that her home life was a mess. Still, she wouldn't take her own bait.

Technically, Alexis never answered my question.

Symbolically, she had answered her own.

———

And then there was Megan.

As part of my smallest-ever class at thirteen students, Megan was often thrust into conversations, debates, and Hot Seat discussions at which she could only roll her eyes. To help offset such tomfoolery was Megan's core group of friends: Elena, Brittney, and Chrissy (who will appear later). Huddled together in a mass of sarcasm and wit, this foursome was the intellectual version of *Mean Girls*. Far from being mean in any way, they just giggled, harrumphed, and sassed their way through that 8th-period honors class. It was one of my favorite classes of my career.

Megan comes from a great family and is a talented singer and musician. Like so many artists, she rarely gave herself the credit she deserved and, almost instinctively, rarely gave others the credit they deserved either. She was the kind of student who may not say something every class period, but, man, when she did, it was profound and smart.

Weeks before graduation, Megan reminded us of such an ability when she answered this question, her last in the Hot Seat.

"I would have to say my grandpop. But, my grandpop passed away so it's kind of hard."

Here we were, an incredibly close class, about to graduate, and Megan got this question and still chose to answer it. Most of us, save for her core group of friends, had no idea about her grandfather's passing. Still, she didn't have to choose this time to talk about his life and legacy. She could have evoked her veto power and moved on.

But she did not.

"Me and my [maternal] grandpop were very, very close. Since my dad doesn't have a relationship with his dad, he was my only grandfather figure. He would have me and my brother sleep over their apartment a lot, and if he knew we wanted to pursue something, he would be the biggest supporter. I specifically remember him getting my sister lots of fashion magazines when she decided to become a fashion merchandiser. My grandpop also practiced parallel parking with my sister for hours when she was getting her license.

"I wish I could remember a lot more stories with my grandpop, but he was diagnosed with lung cancer as I was getting older, and my mom decided it would be best that we didn't see him sick. He is the hardest-working person I will ever know. He started working at 18 and finally retired at 80. He is one of the few people in my life who just knew how to make you feel better without saying a whole lot."

Like I said, sometimes the Hot Seat just finds us, and sometimes we just have to answer. Though she wasn't able to muster much more about her grandpop during her final Hot Seat, we did talk about it years later.

"When I mentioned him in my response, it was the first time I said, 'My grandpop passed away.' It was the first time I recognized it. I kept it all inside because everyone was supposed to be happy to graduate, and happy to meet a new set of challenges in their new schools.

"My grandpop was always so kind and strong-willed, and I knew he wouldn't want me to be upset in a time when no one should be. His passing taught me to enjoy everything life throws at you because every event happens for a reason. Recognizing his passing in the Hot Seat was liberating and the beginning of my healing."

Consider for a second how you may have felt after the recent loss of someone whom you loved dearly. Then, consider how you might choose to cope with that loss. Next, catapult yourself back to your senior year of high school and consider if you would be willing or able to discuss those feelings in front of a jury of your peers.

What Megan did on that day is something none of us will soon forget.

———

Class Reunion with Steve C. (Class of 2002)

Although I don't remember the specifics, here's what I still carry with me after twenty years: vulnerability. I was and am still a very sensitive (39-year-old) kid. For me, one of the toughest parts about high school was having to hide that. It was only cool to not care. I remember being excited for class because I knew I'd have the opportunity to really be myself. It felt safe to be vulnerable. The key to this was that Kulak succeeded in flipping the script. He made the goal to open up and share. That was a success. There was a healthy pressure to do so and I remember there being some awkward and maybe even stressful moments as a group, but it always felt rewarding in the end.

Questions about Identity:

1. Do you judge others by higher or lower standards than you judge yourself?
2. Do you consider yourself a better talker or listener?
3. If you weren't you, would you be friends with you?
4. How much do you really pay attention—in life, in class, in relationships?
5. Are you a good manipulator?

4

REFLECTION

*"What single event, conversation, or decision
has most influenced you so far?"*

This question made it into the book because of its far-reaching implications. Regardless of who was in the chair, the answer was something personal, like most Hot Seat responses. As teachers, we don't always know what our kids are coming to class with unless we take the time to find out. In fact, it was my therapist's idea to put my staff through an opening day exercise during which we all wrote down on sticky notes what we "come to work with" every day and put them in our own brown paper bags. Then, brave teachers shared what's in their bag and how they must compartmentalize their teaching lives against their non-teaching lives, which we can often do because we're grown-ups.

Kids don't necessarily have that luxury.

And even if teenagers do have the emotional intelligence to leave what's in their bags at home, they also have to be willing to share their experience in order for any of us to help them make sense of it. The Hot Seat provided the kind of safety-in-numbers mentality necessary to building a collective trust and, therefore, a collective experience. Answers to this question made the audience reflect on their "single thing" and invited everyone into each other's. As a result, it was often the most emotional Hot Seat question and answer.

Because of the very sensitive nature of this concept, I decided to share my own experience with anxiety, my "single thing." I knew I was an over-thinker, I knew I would feel a sense of pressure in my chest, which I dubbed "the dread," and I knew I would get bummed out from time to time, but I just figured we all did. Moreover, I would rehearse conversations, sometimes dozens of times, that I knew would be contentious, I would get song lyrics stuck in my head (ear-worms) all the time, which I later learned was a classic symptom of anxiety, and I would lose hours of sleep to worry. But like so many of my students, I never talked about it or sought help.

It wasn't until my ex-wife made me aware of how my anxiety was manifesting itself and affecting our marriage that I finally began to look for help. Through a careful combination of regular therapy sessions, a small dose of Lexapro, and a greater sense of self-awareness, I no longer have "the dread" in my chest, or in my life, and I now have strategies in place to help me deal with the anxiety.

My students, on the other hand, likely didn't have such an arsenal at their disposal.

Krista M., a senior in my college prep class, came equipped with one of those stories about her education that gave the profession a black eye. Because of that experience, however, she also had a built-in response to this question.

"I remember sitting in an IEP meeting in 9th grade with my mom and a bunch of other people. [My English teacher] said that I would never be able to grasp such a hard read (*Romeo and Juliet*) so I wouldn't make it in college. My mom spoke up and said maybe the teacher should do her job and work extra with me. This was right before I got diagnosed with ADHD. It was after that conversation that I started to take my medicine because I wanted to prove the teacher wrong."

Before we continue with Krista's response and the support she received from her peers, I feel compelled to address what she shared. First of all, there is no correlation between being able to understand Shakespeare and college readiness. Secondly, if that teacher did have reservations about Krista's college readiness, there is no reason to bring that up out loud with the student present. *In her IEP meeting.* Furthermore, even if that teacher were spot on in her analysis of Krista's ability, the next step would be to work tirelessly with Krista and the Child Study Team to address her deficiencies rather than dismissing her as a failure. Ultimately, this teacher owes Krista an apology, but she has long since retired and lacks the requisite empathy for such a *mea culpa*.

"Then, I finished her general level class with an A, and I astonished her with how well I did with *Romeo and Juliet*. Here's the funny part: I had her again in 11th grade, in college prep, and I no longer had an IEP. I loved rubbing it in her face constantly. There I was, smart all along, and she put me down rather than doing everything in her power to help.

"I think it was that conversation that made me really see what I was capable of. She is the reason I want to be a special education teacher because I know I'll have a better understanding of students and I'll stand up for them, whereas she didn't. At least not in my case."

Now, let's imagine for a second that Krista was never in my class and never had this opportunity to share this experience. Clearly, she had been carrying it around for three years, but no one knew about it, save for the people in that IEP meeting. I'd also be willing to bet that the teacher in question totally forgot about that meeting and what she said in front of Krista until Krista showed back up as a new and improved student two years later.

But Krista didn't forget.

With a platform to share her experience and an audience who applauded her when she was finished, Krista had become a living example of resilience and self-worth. Classmates with similar experiences now felt validated, and shared as much, because someone else spoke up on their behalf. On the other hand, students felt compelled to share experiences to the contrary, experiences with teachers who saw something in them, told them about it, and then cultivated it. By the end of the discussion, the script flipped from Krista being told what she couldn't do to an entire class talking about what they could and *were going* to do.

As an affirmation of this story and so many like it, I reached out to Krista while I wrote this chapter.

"In college, I totally killed anyone's expectations by being on the dean's list every semester, and I had a 3.9 cumulative GPA. I still reflect on the day I shared this because I had to be vulnerable and brave."

She is now an elementary school special education teacher.

I wonder what Shakespeare would say?

Good for you, Krista.

Class Reunion with Joelle M. (Class of 2014)

Individually discussing topics in front of the class provided me with an opportunity to develop a comfortable relationship with my peers, as well as with Mr. Kulak. It also allowed for me to ponder questions I never contemplated asking myself. While I was answering the questions, it was new information that not only my classmates were learning about me, but information I was learning about myself. I am not someone who is comfortable talking about myself in front of other people, let alone twenty of my peers. I would much rather vent on my blog or privately to my sister.

I remember being asked about a lesson I have learned from someone. I began ranting about my mother and how whatever she says has an influence on me. I talked about how she preaches about being an individual. She always says make your own decisions, and do what you want for you. I won't ever forget the moment I said that aloud to my classmates; I feel like it made an imprint. I learned from my mother that I'm an individual who is free to make decisions on her own. One who is not defined by others, or lets other people shape her, well, except for my mom. The Hot Seat helped me develop a concrete ability to speak in front of others, which I am forever grateful for.

Questions about Reflection:

1. What have you been deprived of?
2. What is your life missing right now?
3. What are you too old for right now? Not old enough?
4. What has been your biggest disappointment in life so far? How do you think you've handled it?
5. What is comforting?
6. What is the biggest decision you've had to make so far?
7. What do you most cherish?
8. What would your 18 year old self say to your 8 year old self?
9. How many phases have you gone through in your life?
10. How much of your life has seams (as in gaps)/seems (as in indefinites)?
11. How much of what you have has been earned?
12. Are you ready for what lies after graduation?

13. How many of your friendships have lasted throughout high school and what does that say about such friendships?

14. If I guaranteed you an honest response to any question, what would you ask and of whom?

15. What single event, conversation, or decision has most influenced you so far?

16. What have you learned about yourself in the past two years?

17. To whom do you most look up and why?

18. Is it really possible for any of us to really change?

19. What do you think of the line, "There's nothing worse in life than being ordinary?"

20. Do you consider yourself a hypocrite?

21. Discuss why you think some people are just mean.

5

THE TOOTHPASTE STORY

By the time I was a freshman in high school, I had my career mapped out. I knew I wanted to teach high school English, to coach high school sports, and to write as much as I could. With that knowledge, the rest of high school was really about figuring out *what kind* of teacher I would be.

I am thankful to have attended such a small high school for a myriad of reasons. First, there is no replacement for the intimacy a small school provides. Our graduating class was teeming at 122 students, there was very little transience, and most of us had been together since elementary school. Second, as an athlete, the talent pool against which I had to compete for starting spots was almost non-existent. Kids who went out for a sport in Audubon typically made the team, and most of us played several sports because, again, we sort of had to because there were so few of us. But, finally and most importantly, attending a school of this size does not allow for students to be treated as cogs in a wheel, as clients or constituents. Rather, many members of the teaching and support staff are Audubon graduates, and those who weren't, well, they might as well have been because the school is a family.

I first met John Skrabonja in the fall of 1992 when I walked into his English II (H) class. On his board was a quote of the week, the first of which read, "And summer's lease hath all too short a date," to mourn the passing of another summer. I knew I had heard the line before, but Mr. Skrabonja always provided attribution. In this case, it was a relatively popular writer named Shakespeare. You may have heard of him. We know Krista has.

Sure, Mr. Skrabojna had a traditional bag of tricks: using voices and affectations when reading from *Macbeth*, creating games that were passed off as "fun" but were really rooted in some fundamental grammar practice, owing to unparalleled expertise in his content area, and, above all, making each of us feel like we mattered.

But what Mr. Skrabonja did better than just about every teacher I ever had was to remind us that he was human. He was just a guy who loved English, loved his students, and loved his family, and he was a master at somehow finding a way to combine those three passions into the kind of career I knew I wanted to have.

During an otherwise typical day of teaching and learning, Mr. Skrabonja lost his way. I can't remember the context of the tangent, what, if anything, it had to do with whatever we were studying, or why it stuck with me for the past thirty years, but the "toothpaste story," as I would later dub it for use in my own class, may have been the impetus for the Hot Seat.

"Let me tell you something about my wife that drives me nuts," he started.

Now, it's worth mentioning that Mr. Skrabonja was not the kind of person who would trot out the ol' "women-can't-live-with-em-can't-live-without-them" schtick and pat himself on the back. In fact, providing us with a glimpse into his marriage or parenthood was an anomaly in itself, so no one had any idea what to expect.

"Every time I go into our medicine cabinet to grab the toothpaste, it's always the same thing! It doesn't matter how much toothpaste is left in the tube, my wife squeezes it from the top, so I have to go in every morning and re-squeeze it from the bottom like a *normal* person. Otherwise, the toothpaste just globs together near the cap, so when I squeeze it, it all comes flying out."

Stunned at the intimacy and neurotic nature of the admission, the class sat silent. I think the most common reaction was, "So what? Squeeze the toothpaste your way and move on, dude." Of course, our collective respect for him precluded us from judging or commenting. Or calling him dude.

He went on to explain that marriage is hard and is a constant give and take. The foible was something that irritated him to no end, but it was also emblematic of marriage itself.

And that was it. There was no discussion, no nods of affirmation (because none of us could even begin to imagine what marriage was like), no raised hands or follow-up questions. For whatever reason, Mr. Skrabonja just felt like sharing that tidbit with us, and we were all too eager to accept.

As I worked to shape my own teaching philosophy throughout my career, I always came back to the toothpaste story. I wondered if Mr. Skrabonja purposely offered those rare glimpses into his private life to somehow humanize himself further or if he just, in a more inadvertent but no less purposeful way, felt like complaining about his wife's lack of respect for his preferred dental hygiene practices. In the end, it really didn't matter.

What he taught me was that before I could connect kids to content, I had to connect with my kids. If that meant subtle or overt diversions into my personal life (the aforementioned college breakup), my own foibles (an utter disdain for Michael Jordan or any form of lowest common denominator humor), my non-negotiables (I did not allow the words "gay" or "retarded" to be used derisively in my presence), or anything in between (my love for Pearl Jam and all things baseball), then so be it. Each tangent may have taken us away briefly from the lesson of the day, but each also helped us to circle our own wagons because the kids saw that I trusted them with who I was. In turn, my students were able to trust me and their peers as they sat in the Hot Seat, each telling their own toothpaste stories.

Thank you, John.

6

NEGOTIATION

*"If you could go back in time and change something,
what would it be?"*

I f you ever want to catch a teacher in a bald-faced lie, ask him
if he has favorite students. Whether conditioned or trained,
he'll smirk and assure you teachers don't have favorites because
it's our responsibility to teach and care for all of our students.

But two things can be true.

While I may not have a constantly updating scoreboard
keeping track of favorite students, this book would not be possible
without the kind of authentic, transcendent relationships I have
developed with *certain* students.

So, yes, I, too, am a liar. I have plenty of favorites.

Chrissy D. is one of them.

After she graduated, I remained in contact with Chrissy during her pre-service teaching career. Whether she was asking for advice on a paper or on her resume, I was honored to be part of her journey on the way to becoming an English teacher herself. I knew she would make an excellent one and that she didn't need my help as much as she thought she did.

In my class, she sat in the back corner and was part of the aforementioned smallest group I ever had, which allowed for the kind of deep, meaningful Hot Seat sessions that were sometimes harder to facilitate among larger groups. She was wickedly sarcastic, often eye-rolling, and always on point. She is also unique in that she remembered her question and answer with such precision that her inclusion in the book wasn't as much considered as it was mandatory.

What's important about this question is that its responses were so varied, so personal, that I could have used it with every student. Reflection and self-awareness take years of maturity, the likes of which often don't develop until well into adulthood. Teenagers aren't typically asked to reflect on a life too nascent to warrant the kind of depth we might find in someone, say, twice their age. Moreover, answers to this question often included some variation of "nothing." Such kids were either so self-aware that they accepted that their life is their life and to change it would be unnatural, or too immature, intellectually or emotionally, that they couldn't come up with something to change.

But kids like Chrissy, and so many like her, were almost waiting for someone to ask her this question.

"I would go back to the middle of 7th grade and change the way I carried myself. At the time, I just moved from Florida to

Audubon. I was so lonely and desperate for friends that I let kids walk all over me. The kids at the new school would throw away my lunch, make fun of me.

"I had this pair of shoes that I loved (they were black flats with multi-colored hearts on them) but ultimately I ended up throwing them away because the girls laughed at them. I failed classes and stopped talking to my mom (who is my favorite person in the world). I always loved school, but for those five months, there would be days I refused to go. I made myself small for people who were never going to like me anyway. If I could go back in time, I would have stuck up for myself."

I made myself small for people who were never going to like me anyway.

If you're a teacher and you're reading this, you just thought of someone who Chrissy reminds you of. If you're a parent and you're reading this, you're praying this identity crisis doesn't befall your own child. If you're neither and you're reading this, you're picturing that one kid with whom you went to school that you know felt this way. Heck, you may have *contributed* to making her feel this way. Or worse: You still feel this way about *yourself.*

"The Hot Seat was the first time I told people about the way I was treated when I moved here. And that I did have something to say worth listening to. At the time, I was still being walked on by people I considered to be my friends, but it was the first step I took to stick up for myself. It was a lesson that was difficult to learn and one that I didn't realize I was still learning at the time of my question. But it did get me to reflect on my experiences in a public, vulnerable, cathartic way. And I am very grateful for my time in that bright orange chair; it was a rite of passage and an experience worth talking about (preferably in a public setting using as little "ums" as possible)."

For Chrissy, this question and response represented a catharsis. With graduation peeking out from behind the curtain, she took this opportunity to assure herself that her life's next big change, college, was not going to follow the same script as the one she used in middle school. Then, extrapolate that out several years, and we can see her teaching style begin to take shape right there in the Hot Seat.

Like so many of my former students who went on to become teachers, Chrissy adapted the Hot Seat and made it her own.

"I know you're supposed to live without regrets, but teaching 7th grade now has given me what I like to think of as a re-do. In many ways, I see myself in some of the students I teach now. I see the anxiety of trying to fit in, saying the wrong things, figuring myself out. And now I get to give my students advice I wish someone gave me (which as one would expect is not always taken).

"I started doing this thing in my life called 'radical vulnerability' in which I am open and honest about the way I feel and I've been encouraging my kids to do the same. I've lost interest in trying to be cool, and I fully embrace being the nerdy, 'let's talk about life' teacher. I try to incorporate materials and opportunities for my kids (and myself) to be vulnerable. For example, every January, regardless of what grade I am teaching that year, I do an assignment called 'A Year in Review' where I ask students to reflect on the previous year through the lens of their social, family, and academic life in addition to talking about where they need to grow and parts about them that they need/want to change. It's not quite the Hot Seat, but I think the idea behind it is Hot Seat inspired."

For Chrissy, the Hot Seat provided her the opportunity to say the quiet part out loud. Like most teenagers, hers was an internal struggle between accepting who she was and rejecting what *other people* thought she was. A powerful self actualization she now encourages from her own students, several of whom are mini Chrissys just waiting for someone to ask and to listen.

———

Class Reunion with Markie V. (Class of 2011)

The Hot Seat, in a literal sense, made you sweat. The point was to make us think hard and give an honest answer to serious, sometimes emotional, questions. The methodology behind this was simple, but effective. Ironically, mulling over the thought of actually changing because of the Hot Seat makes me feel like I am in the Hot Seat right now, chewing at the unsaid words in my mouth, wondering about the appropriateness of them. The Hot Seat itself wasn't a beacon of knowledge that made me learn something about myself; it was a symbol of change. The change to become the person I knew I was capable of being.

Questions about Negotiation:

1. Is the unknown more terrifying or exhilarating?
2. Who is a "bigger" person, the one who apologizes or the one who accepts?
3. Is most betrayal planned or accidental?
4. What is more exciting, anticipation or realization?
5. What does everyone deserve?
6. Is it true that while the cat's away the mice will play?
7. Are you capable of murder?
8. What could the world do without?
9. If given a choice, would you rather endure emotional or physical pain?
10. Is there a difference between a reason and an excuse?
11. Is there a difference between accepting and settling?
12. Give me a good example of an exception to the rule.
13. Are you more likely to cover for someone or have someone cover for you?
14. What's your favorite place in the world and why?
15. If you had memory issues and could pick one thing to remember/forget what or who would it be?
16. Why?
17. What makes you laugh?
18. Is it better to be honest and hurt someone or lie and protect him/her?
19. What is your personal meaning of life?
20. What is the most important thing in your life right now?

21. To what do you most look forward?

22. What is one of the biggest problems facing a person your age and/or gender right now?

23. Recall your first day as a student (in high school) and describe that feeling or walk us through the day. Now put yourself in your first college class. Do you think the feeling will be the same?

24. Is it more difficult/frightening to look ahead or to look back?

25. What has been the biggest disappointment in your life so far? How do you think you handled it?

7

LEGACY

"If you were reincarnated, what would you come back as?"

S ome 25 years ago, this is the first chapter I wrote about The Hot Seat. What started as a relatively simple question and answer turned into a friendship with its responder, Kaylee C. Her response was the first time a student responded with a kind of depth and maturity I wasn't expecting when I came up with the idea. And it was at that moment that I knew The Hot Seat was going to become something special.

"I think I would come back as a tree," Kaylee started. "Because then I would be around for years and years to see how the world changes."

Kaylee will always hold a special place in the Hot Seat

pantheon of responses. A whip-smart girl of the people, there was nothing Kaylee couldn't do. She cheered, she wrote, she spoke French, she volunteered, she sang.

She was only a sophomore when she answered this question.

Normally, answers to this question, particularly from my boys, were predictable. Visceral. Immature. Such answers were just as valid, despite their relatively flimsy foundation, because they were, for the most part, genuine. I never wanted kids to concoct some Hot Seat alter-ego for my benefit because, invariably, doing so would create a totally disingenuous answer to which the audience would react anyway.

And despite the safety I could provide during the Hot Seat, there was no escaping the court of public opinion.

Back to Kaylee.

As I mentioned, Kaylee and I are still close, so when I reached out to her to confirm that transcendent answer, it came as no surprise that her memory of the experience was full of clarity and detail.

"My first chance at the Hot Seat was in your Honors English II class my sophomore year. Rarely am I at a loss for words, but you asked a question about conformity that, on the spot, I just could *not* wrap my head around, so I sat there and just shrugged my shoulders until you finally let me go back to my seat.

"I also recall after that first round of the Hot Seat with all of your classes you mentioned that there was only one person that didn't have a grade, and I knew it was me. I'm also picturing myself in dark blue cargo pants and a white, short-sleeved v-neck shirt both from The Weathervane (so year 2000) that first time on the Hot Seat.

"My second time in the Hot Seat, I was asked about reincarnation and what I would want to be if I were reincarnated. I'm sure what was only a few seconds seemed like a lifetime to my 16-year-old self. Your classroom was in the top corner of 'A Building' then, and I remember looking out of the windows where those beautiful old trees were swaying in the breeze behind the memorial. And then I finally blurted out *a tree!*"

It was an honest, if not panicked, response to an admittedly existential question, especially for a high school sophomore, but I knew its depth was genuine and its implications were more far-reaching than she knew at the time. Her answer also changed what I expected from student responses because in those early days I was content if students said *anything*. After her answer, I became convinced that my students were capable, and often willing, of so much more than surface-level-get-me-out-of-this-chair responses. So it's because of Kaylee that I started to push, started to ask more follow-up questions, and started to marvel at and comment on how impressive my kids were.

For Kaylee, the response continues to resonate as she reflects on her life since that day in the Hot Seat.

"After high school, I was off to Ithaca for college. A four-hour drive doesn't make it easy to come home too often, but it was still close enough to pack up and visit when I felt like it. A semester in LA was an adventure on the West Coast, but it goes by so fast -- so does almost 20 years post that semester in LA. After college, I spent a little time in Syracuse before running away to France for eight months.

"After that, the wandering was more in my career choices than in my actual location. Freelance journalism, unpaid internships, substitute teaching by day, restaurants on the side, they filled up my time after my return from France in 2008 until I started working in restaurants full-time in 2010. I was good at organizing parties and planning schedules and managing staff, but I knew it wasn't what I wanted to be doing.

"I started at Anthropologie in October of 2012 working in events and loyalty marketing. I wasn't exactly setting the world on fire, but I didn't hate my job, which is more than I could say for some of my peers! And while I knew I wouldn't make a career out of event planning (or working in retail for that matter), I couldn't have gotten to my current position without it.

"In 2018, I moved back up to Ithaca to work at my alma mater as an event planner and volunteer manager for our alumni relations team. Shortly after, I made the leap into fundraising, and for the first time, I didn't question the work I was doing. At the very end of 2021, with an abundance of higher-ed institutions in the Philly area, I used my network and new skills to land a job at a university (Rowan) that's been in my backyard this whole time."

Obviously, this level of reflection and self-awareness can only come after years of living a life for which Kaylee laid her own roots. At the time of her answer, Kaylee would have told you that she just "really loves trees." But that's the difference between a wide-eyed teen and a reflective grown-up.

"In all of my adventures and among all of my jobs, I've met

some of the absolute best people, and though it may not be so obvious, I was spending all that time working on my roots. Now that I've planted myself back home, like those big old trees, my roots will run much deeper and much wider than my little plot of land in South Jersey."

"My roots will reach Ithaca, once a town held up by college memories but is now home to some of my closest friends. They'll reach Boston and Maine, where my best college gal pals live with their husbands and babies. They'll reach France, where a sweet family took me in for a school year and let me watch over their children. From France, they'll extend to England, where other assistants now live after our experience teaching English to French students. To the South, they'll reach Honduras, where an intelligent friend is now working as a Foreign Service Officer. To the west, they'll reach California where I still keep in touch with co-workers from an internship and college classmates who made the leap to the Pacific to work in Hollywood. And, of course, my roots will be many the closer I am to home.

"On second thought, let's forget reincarnation. I'm pretty sure I'm already one lucky tree."

While I'm sure such is the case for other Hot Seat veterans, Kaylee's answer ended up being reverse-engineered. Her answer applied to that spring day in 2000, but because of the life she lived since then, its metaphor and application extend to this day. In fact, so many of my conversations with graduates about The Hot Seat have included references to how a particular question has "followed" them or how "they still remember" their answer because it's still true today.

Like Kaylee and her tree, each planted roots long before they knew where those roots would take them.

———

Class Reunion with Emma S. (Class of 2014)

It was an effective activity because not only did it challenge us to speak in front of our peers, but also it provoked us to truly consider our thoughts and feelings as we responded to a question without much time to prepare. This helped greatly with skills necessary for interviews, college, and beyond, while also consistently proving to be an interesting activity that students looked forward to on Fridays.

I'm quite the talker and always have something to say, so my most fond memory of the Hot Seat is the idea of the overall discussions that it instigated. I loved listening to people's responses, especially when the questions were very personal; however, even more so, I loved putting in my own two cents whether I agreed with the speaker or not. The Hot Seat provided a safe yet fiery environment where debates and discussions were welcomed with open arms and allowed each student to express their thoughts on a subject without judgment.

Upon being asked the question, "Would you rather endure emotional or physical pain," I was surprised by my own answer: emotional. This triggered an interesting discussion in class, as in years past most people had normally chosen physical when posed the same question. My rationale behind my choice was that while physical pain does end, I would not be who I am today without having gone through the emotional pain I have endured. It made me realize that I truly appreciate all of my experiences in life, both good and bad, and I can say that I have learned from every one while also not letting any bad experiences define who I am or stop me from being who I want.

Questions about Legacy:

1. If you were reincarnated, what would you come back as?
2. Who would you want to eulogize you and what would you want him/her to say?
3. When you leave high school, how do you think you'll be remembered? How should you be remembered?
4. What is one lesson you have been taught throughout your life that you will always remember?
5. What is your favorite high school memory and why?

8

FLIPPING THE SCRIPT

K aren Dyer was dying.

No amount of Ice Bucket Challenge videos, Lou Gehrig speeches, or rereads of *Tuesdays With Morrie* was going to change that. She had ALS, or rather ALS had her; she deteriorated very quickly, and she was dying.

A former student, Erin B., responded to my Facebook post about the book with: *Is there any way you could reach out to Mrs. Dyer about this? She loved the idea of Hot Seat and loved actually being in the Hot Seat even more.*

When I started putting out feelers for the book based on student experience in the Hot Seat, I hadn't even thought about including a chapter about a colleague's day in my class. I was disappointed in myself for not considering her Hot Seat question and response, and the permanent mark it left on the eighteen people who were lucky enough to witness it.

Luckily, I still had some time.

Erin wrote in past tense because by this time, around June of 2015, Karen had been forced to leave the classroom, despite vowing to finish one more year. The ALS was simply too powerful. As I read it now, the fact that Erin used the past tense is even more sadly prescient.

I emailed Karen early in the summer of 2015 to set up a time to meet with her. I told her about Erin's request and about the fact that so many kids, especially a very close group of amazing girls, had such an affinity for her. We both admitted that we couldn't quite recall the question or the answer she gave, but we both remembered the resounding feeling of quiet that followed her response. She told me that she was off to Hawaii for a couple of weeks to celebrate her 40th anniversary with her husband, Bruce, and that she had a couple of quick jaunts locally after that, so she would be happy to meet any time that was mutually conducive.

I didn't respond for another two months.

While I did get bogged down in typical workday nonsense, I'm certain I could have gotten back to her sooner. When I did, my message was brief and too impersonal.

"Didn't forget about you! Just really busy!" I wrote.

How insensitive.

I was so busy that I couldn't consider a person who would never again know what busy felt like. Finally, we had this email exchange.

Saturday August 1st, 2015

Karen: I'm home and rested. Call sometime. I'm pretty free.

Friday September 4th, 2015

Me: Are you available this afternoon?

Karen: Yes. What time were you thinking? I usually nap for a while, somewhere between 12 and 4. Were you thinking after school? Does 3ish work for you? Bruce has meetings after school, so I need to be sure to be awake when you arrive. Let me know. I can adjust my sleep time. No problem.

Me: How about a call? I don't want to interrupt your nap!

Karen: I can't talk on the phone anymore. In person, I have to use my new voice via my tablet. It's OK to come today, just let me know the time so I can plan.

Me: I can come by around 3 for sure. What's your address?

———

As I knew her professionally, Karen was deeply devoted to her students. She taught American Literature and ESL courses, each with the same dignified, thoughtful approach. Like most educators, Karen typically referred to her students as "my kids," but in her case, the phrase spoke more to pride than to pomp and circumstance. She did everything deliberately: speaking, walking, listening, teaching, and she was quick to speak up at a department meeting if she felt like yet another administrative edict was unwarranted. She had frizzy, whitening hair, she wore glasses, and her sweaters looked homemade.

In preparation for student presentations, her preferred form of assessment, she baked for her kids. In fact, like any Pavlovian experiment subject, her kids can likely tell you what they were studying based on what they remember eating during the lesson. Maybe it's in reverse, but you get the point.

When I asked Erin to elaborate on her time spent with Karen, she became the first participant in a virtual Hot Seat. She responded via Facebook:

"The main thing is just that I've never met a teacher, or anyone for that matter, who truly loves her job as much as she did. She saw the absolute best in every single one of her students. Some kids in our class would present total shit, and everyone knew they did it the night prior at 2 in the morning, but she would sit there and try to really understand what the students' point was. I've had a ton of teachers in my life, but none of them cared about her students like she did. I just love Karen," she wrote.

Later, I spoke with another one of Karen's former students, Val P., who echoed Erin's sentiments.

"A lot of teachers out there just dismiss you if you don't understand, if you did an assignment incorrectly, or have a question. I've had a lot of teachers in my life that just simply didn't feel like arguing with me, so they would just agree to shut me up, and that would show up in my work. I feel like I'd be doing things wrong but some teachers would just let me be because I asked entirely too many questions and argued.

"She was different. In class, and Erin can attest to this, I would argue with her about rules and words and things of that nature, and she would never raise her voice at me or even get aggravated. She would just always calmly answer my questions and basically always put me in my place.

"She also was very down to earth. She was very understanding of other school work and just personal issues of other kids, and she tried her best to be a friend to you. That's what I love the most. I could literally talk to her about anything, and she gave the best advice. She's just the most genuine person I know, and I look up to her in so many ways."

Two words, *love* and *forever*, resonated with me long after I talked to Erin and Val. Regardless of context, the two are often inextricably linked and are rarely used in reference to a teacher. Kids will remember teachers, can relate to teachers, and might emulate teachers, but in this case, I believe that Erin, and so many like her, actually feel a form of love for Karen. It may not be the kind she feels for her parents or her sister. It is certainly not what she feels for her best friend or her husband. It is, instead, the kind of love you feel for someone because you spent a specific kind of quality time with her that you will never spend with someone else. Whether that time was spent learning, laughing, sharing, or listening to her story, Karen's "kids," regardless of their DNA, love her.

———

When I arrived at her house that afternoon, I expected sadness to greet me at the door, as if I were meeting with ALS itself, not the person it currently inhabited, so I prepared for the worst. The problem is it is impossible to gauge what the worst is without any frame of reference.

Oddly, I didn't find myself nervous as I walked up the path to her front door. Because I hadn't seen her since I left Audubon in June of 2014, I had already superimposed that version of Karen over whatever manifestation I was about to meet. In this way, I could guard myself against the possibility that I would first be greeted by her hospice nurse, by her beleaguered husband, or, worse, by a shell of herself. Still, I was thinking about myself, not about her.

After I knocked unnecessarily softly, she answered the door without a word. I knew she had lost her ability to speak, but the juxtaposition between my effusive greeting and her wordless one was palpable. Shortly thereafter, I had to gird myself for communicating through a combination of my questions, her grunts, and the mechanized voice coming from inside her iPad. Using a pen designed for the app, Karen was able to communicate her thoughts by dragging the pen over the keyboard at warp speed. Then, the app would spit back those thoughts, although they were often only rough estimates of what Karen intended, in a generic, female robot voice. Her right hand never moved, in stark contrast to the speed at which her left hand moved to trace the pen over the letters on the keyboard.

Physically, Karen looked like the person with whom I had taught just over a year ago. She didn't move with any noticeable struggle or pain, her laugh was the same, and she had a powerful brightness to her eyes, which I either hadn't noticed before or was her body's way of reminding visitors that she was still in there. She did wipe saliva from the corner of her mouth often, she shook, she sighed, and she was tired.

The room, positioned at the very front of the house, didn't look makeshift or clinical. Where I thought I would find a hospital bed, I instead saw a single desk fan blowing warm air, boxes of papers, books, and folders, and a sewing machine with partially stitched swathes. I wondered if this was what the house always looked like or if these were the remnants of previously planned projects that would now go unfinished.

Before we started, I remember thinking that she had ALS, but ALS didn't have her.

Yet.

"I started when I was 24 at a residential school for the deaf. Kids were not close to families often but (were) to people at school because we could communicate. I had no kids then, so they were *my kids*. When I came back to teaching, *my kids* were pretty much grown, and again, I had *my kids* at school. I just talked about this yesterday; I don't know how people have little ones and teach! I know I wouldn't have been happy or satisfied in either place. To me, they are both full-time jobs. And demand full attention and caring.

"[And then] ESL is a whole other animal. I was so close to those kids because I had them year after year."

When we reflected on Karen's turn to take the Hot Seat, I treated her like I would any of my students. Still, neither of us could remember her question.

"I got two questions because I didn't like the first question.

What year was it? 2014? The first question was something about the hardest thing I had to face, and I brought up my son's death, which most of the kids knew about vaguely. Then it all came flooding back, as it can do at any time.

"I think no matter what the next question was, it would have been tough. I might have teared up then but I think I got my composure. The next question was about my other kids, the students, at least in my interpretation. I knew then that something serious was going on with me even though I didn't have a diagnosis. I was fearful of losing my ability to do the job I love."

We agreed, in hindsight, that the question and answer really didn't matter. I think Karen asked to sit in the Hot Seat on that day because she knew she wouldn't be able to by the following fall. I think Karen responded with such stripped-down honesty because she knew there was no longer a reason to separate the teacher from the person. I think she used "my kids" interchangeably because she really did not see a difference between her students and her biological children.

I think she sat in the Hot Seat to say goodbye.

Those kids, the ones she calls *my kids*, sat in silence as Karen dabbed away runaway tears from her cheeks. Those kids used every ounce of strength to not give in to their own impending tears. Many of them failed. Those kids still talk about Karen, her class, and her compassion in a way that suggests complete reverence.

Without question, Karen's turn in the Hot Seat reflects the indelible power a teacher can have on "her kids." Their words on her behalf may serve as a eulogy to which only the kids in the room that day can relate, but anyone who has a Karen Dyer in her life can appreciate the power of empathy, of humanity, of *love*, and of *forever*.

9

IDENTITY PART II

"Is there a difference between being lonely and being alone?"

This question *seems* fairly simple. If I were answering my own question, I would argue that loneliness is an emotional state while being alone is a physical state. I would also add that many of us, like myself, value alone time. Away from the pressures of, frankly, other people, we often do our best thinking, relaxing, reflecting, writing. Because educators dedicate our lives to other people's kids, aloneness is rarely actualized. Sometimes we sit down in an empty classroom only to have it filled with a kid in crisis, with a kid in need of extra help, or with a colleague who needs to vent or celebrate. In each of these cases, we willingly accept, and often revel in, the fact that people want to be around us, that they value us, and that we matter.

On the other hand, sometimes all those components can be in

place, and we still feel a sense of isolation or detachment. Therein, I would argue, is the difference. I'll let Tyler C., a senior, explain.

"Until this year, I was, like, a shut-in who did not want to deal with the world. I was scared of trying to talk to anyone for fear of mistakenly saying something wrong, so I stayed home for the most part—besides going to school. I did that for three years of my high school career while hiding behind my writing. I was able to get my thoughts across through paper, but not through in person. I've always looked at being alone as a way to step back and improve without interference.

"Lonely is a different story. Someone can be in love, have everything they want, and still be lonely. Being lonely is a state of mind, and unfortunately, a lot of us may have been there. But that can't make us shut out the world. At least it shouldn't. Sometimes life happens, and it all comes back down to communication."

Tyler first came to me by way of our high school newspaper, *The Parrot*, for which I was the advisor. By his own admission, he was awkward, thoughtful, and consumed by gaming. But there was also a side to him that could only be seen through his writing, as he mentioned during his response. He wrote fantasy, horror, and shape-shifting fiction, most of which he would share with me. When he wasn't creating fictitious worlds, we would often compare notes about video games like *Resident Evil* and *Silent Hill*. We remain friends to this day.

The question, he said, "resonates with me as life moves forward" because the often claustrophobic walls of a high school as small as ours don't lend themselves to kids like Tyler finding a social group to call his own. As a result, life can often be a battle between wanting to fit in and wanting to get out. It's kids like Tyler for whom society has made the blurry line between loneliness and being alone indecipherable.

By the time Tyler answered this question, he was both a senior and in year two as a member of the newspaper staff. In September, Tyler asked me to consider him for editor-in-chief. My first reaction was to thank him for his interest but to pass. While Tyler loved to write, he didn't necessarily have the requisite leadership or technical writing skills to tackle such a demanding job. My former editors-in-chief were charismatic, understood the nuances of writing, and could convey that to their peers without judgment. I wasn't sure Tyler fit the bill.

I had other candidates in mind, but the main difference between them and Tyler was he *asked* for the position. How often do high school seniors *ask* for more work? How often is that extra work then scrutinized by the entire building? Moreover, he had a year of experience on staff, he made it clear he was interested in writing beyond high school, and he was stepping outside his comfort zone, so I named him editor-in-chief the next day.

His response to the question, however, "resonates" with me as well because he was able to neatly compartmentalize the distinction between loneliness and being alone from a place within the question, not removed from it. Had a more outgoing, self-confident student answered this question he may have come off as disingenuous or even self-righteous. Unless we have lived in a place of utter loneliness, even if that place seems manufactured or societally imposed, we really can't lend any credence to what that feels like. We can guess. We can try to feel some level of empathy. We can even pretend. But we won't really understand.

Similarly, for those of us who thrive among company, who seek out opportunities to be part of a larger community, who feel completely at ease as a face among many, we can't do justice as the voice of the alone. For us, being alone is terrifying. To whom do we speak? From where do we find peace and comfort? How do we fill the widening gaps in time and space? The answer is, quite simply, we don't.

The same cannot be said for those who go out of their way to find some "alone time." For that reason, I would much rather hear the response of a person who, like me, looks forward to the serenity of aloneness. Unfortunately, I don't choose the questions based on the student's personality. The student chooses the question and, like is so often the case, the question finds the student.

Class Reunion with Jeri F. (Class of 2008)

My question was to choose one word to describe yourself. I chose "actor," because I was figuring out who I was, and that I would either become a chameleon around certain groups or wear a mask around others because I didn't know who I was, and I didn't want to be judged for who I knew I was.

I got really good at putting on faces. Sarcastic enough in some crowds, quiet enough, smart enough, aloof enough and then, with a little group of friends, "me" enough. That got me through high school and college well enough. [Eventually] I found that being myself all of the time was a lot of fun. After years of hiding it or not speaking up about certain things, I still sometimes feel like an imposter with my true personality – when that happens, I just need to remind myself that that is who I am.

I feel like after becoming a mom, the need to be as authentic as I possibly can has become one of the most important things I could do for myself so that my kids know that it's okay to be who they are, no matter how weird or quirky that may be.

Questions about Identity (cont'd):

1. Knowing yourself, what is the one thing in life which you know you can't handle?
2. Outside of a parent, choose the one person who has helped you become who you are.
3. Do you find yourself to be more anxious or relaxed?
4. Do you typically finish what you start?
5. What is your worst quality?
6. What do you most worry about and why?

10

DEATH

"If you knew you were going to die,
what would you want to have accomplished?"

I nevitably, one of the themes that commanded the most vocal
response is death. Whether we want to admit it or not, we all
have some anxiety about death, and I thought it would be interesting to see how pronounced that anxiety is in the teenage mind.
This question also lent itself to a clearer picture of teen
psychology because it forced kids to prioritize necessity over
desire or vice versa. Furthermore, the answers were often gender
specific in that girls had romantic ideas about their final days and
guys had more primal, selfish responses. Ultimately, the beauty of
the question was in its immediacy. I told the kids, because they
always asked, that they had one year from the date of the question. This gave them a frame of reference through which they

could answer a bit more concretely. Kids started by saying, "I don't know" or "I don't like this question," but once the seed was planted, and it included an expiration date, they opened up.

As difficult a topic as death is, many kids welcomed the opportunity to discuss it openly, often for the first time, because it had already affected their lives in some way. One of the most resounding answers came from Kim L. (2000). For whatever reason, her response came rather easily to her, and the class seemed to feed off her openness.

She said that she wouldn't really change anything about her life. She felt like goals that she set for herself without knowing she would die shouldn't be compromised because of an ominous date. Kim wanted to earn a college degree, and while we all agreed that would be unattainable in a year, her desire to get a college education didn't and couldn't be measured in time or with a piece of paper. Kim shared a common desire that many high school students were tentative to express in front of people: the prestige and honor that comes with a college degree. Many high schoolers are too consumed by their present to consider the weight of their future. The rare perspective that Kim expressed, even in the face of fictional, certain death, made her unique in a way that should be celebrated.

The most intriguing discussion, although it eventually spiraled into a public flogging, evolved from a comment I made in one of our typical follow-up discussions. When the question was turned back on me, I said without hesitation, "I would marry my girl-friend and have a child as soon as possible." The answer rolled off my tongue with such genuine sincerity that it never occurred to me that it might be an unpopular answer. Jaws dropped, pens dropped, and my approval rating, most certainly, dropped.

As had become the case so often with the Hot Seat, my responses carried with them an immediate disclaimer. This answer was no different. In the face of so many angry onlookers, I explained that I couldn't wait to become a husband and father, and that if faced with the possibility that I may not have the opportunity to realize such a dream with the woman I was convinced I would marry, I would want to expedite matters. While that calmed some of the less fanatical students, it did not stop the inquisition.

"That is the most selfish thing I have ever heard…what about the baby who will grow up without a father? That is so selfish."

Nicole M. was an opportunistically outspoken young woman in my senior class who never passed up the chance to contribute to post-response discussions, though her own Hot Seat responses were often very guarded.

"And what about the wife you'll leave behind to raise your kid? What do you expect from her?" Support for Nicole came in the form of Brandon R., a student who was far and away one of the brightest and one of my favorites.

"And what do you tell your wife to tell your child about you when he or she is old enough? 'Well, dear, your father was going to die, and he just had to have you?' C'mon, Mr. Kulak, that's no way for a child to be raised," came more vitriol from Christine L.

"What if your girlfriend doesn't want to marry a dying man and have his kid?" came a snide, but no less relevant, remark from Dave D. in the back of the room.

The class ended abruptly as the bell interrupted our debate, but it was also a Friday afternoon, which meant that every kid in the class had the weekend to consider, brood, and gather more ammunition for the coming Monday.

On Monday, I spoke to a student in that class, Ryan B., who hung out in my room during his 4th-period study hall. He told me that the Hot Seat question was a topic of discussion at his house on that same Friday night. Apparently, two students whom I did not teach were at Ryan's house that night. The question came up, and what ensued was a passionate and angry debate that almost ended in fisticuffs.

The two kids who I did not teach and who did not hear the discussion saw nothing wrong with my answer. Ryan remained steadfast that my answer was sexist and selfish. Thankfully, the argument did not escalate into violence, but I have to admit that a wry smile did cross my face as I pictured the events of that evening. Kids were not only talking about a discussion in my class but also reporting back to me days later. Remember, too, that I was all of 23 years old at this point, and without a frame of reference or semester under my belt, I was willing to accept any small victory.

It was then that I realized that the Hot Seat had arrived.

Later that day, during my admittedly rehearsed apology, I explained in as much detail as possible that it was not my intention to incite a riot, but to impart a bit of humanity. I said that nothing would be done without the consent of my girlfriend, who I had assumed, albeit presumptuously, would be of the same mind on the issue. I considered taking out a picture of her to add to her otherwise anonymous persona, but I thought better of it. I went on to explain that having a child is the only thing in life that I really *wanted*, that I could do without the rest. If presented with the difficult circumstance that death may come before I had the opportunity, it wouldn't change the fact that I wanted to be a dad.

It was then that facial expressions turned from outright anger to, well, at least veiled anger. I explained that knowing I was going to die wasn't the catalyst for marriage or fatherhood–love and devotion were. I told them I was confident that my wife would carry on my memory through pictures, stories, and the aid of other family members. I wanted to give my wife and my family a piece of me before I left. I wanted to experience marriage and fatherhood if only for a moment.

It took some work, but most of the crowd finally came back to the home team's side. At that moment, I was so proud of my kids, and not because my little speech had affected thirty angry teenagers (it was a *massive* class), but because those thirty angry teenagers were willing to be part of a difficult discussion, one that they themselves had co-authored.

In the end, this question and its responses were not about death at all.

They were about life.

———

Class Reunion with Megan C. (Class of 2014)

When I got my question (*"If I guaranteed you an honest response to any question, what would you ask and of whom?"*), I immediately thought of my father who was in and out of my life. I looked up with tears in my eyes and said that I would ask if he really loves me. Although that went to a serious place really quickly, it showed just how comfortable I was around my peers in that class even early in the year.

You never knew what kind of question you were going to get and I loved that. It kept the emotions real every time. That seat changed the whole atmosphere of the class, and I feel that no matter who sat in that chair, it was all eyes on them, and we supported them whether it was a funny question, a serious question, whatever. That question I received that day led to an amazing senior essay that Kulak and I worked on, which helped get me into the university that I so badly wanted. That seat led to great things, and I hope everyone got their moment like that.

Questions about Death:

1. If you knew you were going to die, what would you want to have accomplished?
2. Would you want to know how and when you were to die?
3. What happens after we die?

11

LOVE

*"Is it true that it is better to have loved and lost
than to never have loved at all?"*

You can imagine the chuckles, sideways glances, and impassioned responses this question warranted. The reason I like this question so much is kids had no idea what they are getting themselves into. They knew they loved their parents, their dog, and their friends, but they couldn't really tell if what they felt for someone else was true love. If we're being honest, there are plenty of grown-ups who still struggle with this concept.

Some kids were convinced they were currently in love, others seemed convinced they were once in love, still others swore they never wanted to be in love, and the rest were afraid to admit allegiance to any of those categories. Of course, making this concept even more confusing for teens is the perpetual armwrestling match between love and lust.

When I first asked this question to a chatty group of seniors in 2001, most answered it without really thinking it through. And, as usual, most of the earnest responses came from girls.

"Without a doubt to have never loved at all because then you have no idea what you're missing. See, if you never had it then you don't get involved in those conversations about it with your friends, you don't get all swept up in the thing, and then you don't have to worry about it ending crappy," offered Stacey M. who would easily be an inaugural member of the Hot Seat Hall of Fame. "Guys suck and that's that."

After reminding her that I am part of the "sucky" gender, to which she eloquently referred, I asked the class if teenagers had become numb to the idea of love. Was it true, I wondered aloud, that they have been desensitized to or have become disinterested in love?

"It takes too much energy to have a boyfriend or girlfriend. It's easier without attachments. I'm not saying that's what I think, but that's what most people do nowadays," offered Rebecca C.

"But you guys have to admit that when you are in love, however long or short, it is pretty sweet," came the voice of Charlie D. Thankfully, some testosterone.

"Like how you look forward to seeing or talking to that person all day. Or how you see yourself as a better person because of the other. I have been crapped on before, but I still wouldn't trade the feeling of comfort or security or whatever that I had before I got dumped. No way."

I felt like it was time for a trademark Kulak anecdote, so I told the class that I was going through the most difficult time in my life. I explained that my college girlfriend's father died shortly after she had been offered a job near where we both went to college. When her father died, she returned to her family's home in North Jersey to mourn and never came back. I admitted to the class that I couldn't get past some of the things we shared, the plans we made, the people we were together.

"Yeah, but seriously, when you think about her and miss her, are you, like, resentful or just sad?" asked Laurie M.

"Honestly, Laur, it depends. I guess I am never resentful, but sometimes I wish I hadn't spent that time with her only to have it end in confusion and heartache. If I had stayed single during college, maybe this wouldn't have been so hard. Well, obviously, it wouldn't have been, I guess."

"I know what you mean, but you obviously miss her, so what she means to you kinda is more than what she doesn't mean to you. You know what I mean?"

I did understand what she was saying, and it was all at once amazing and humbling that such advice or perspective came from a seventeen-year-old whom I was trying to help, not vice versa.

"I think the point is, we are all able to sit and make judgments from a removed point of view, but when it comes down to it, we'd all like to be in love at some point or another. That's what life's all about, right? I mean, if we don't take risks and give everything we have to a person, then what else is there?" I finished.

As easy as it was for me to pontificate on love and loss, it was just as difficult for kids to process what I was saying. Each of them participated in that discussion through the lens of their own experience with love, often based on how love played out in their own homes. By the end, most were able to accept that there are other ways to consider something as heavy as love despite what they thought they already knew. It was also crucial, as it was during any conversation of this magnitude, that I convinced my kids that I was by no means an expert or a final authority on anything we discussed. I assured them that just because I'm older, though only by 6 or 7 years, and can talk about these issues with perspective doesn't make me right.

Because the Hot Seat was *never* about being right. Rather, it was just about *being*.

———

Questions about Love:

1. Are you marriage material?
2. You are asked to choose between a soulmate and no close friends or several close friends and no soulmate. Which would you choose and why?
3. How important is it for you to "find someone?"
4. At what age do you think it's possible to fall in love?
5. Is it more important to love or to be loved?
6. Should there be an age requirement for dating?
7. Why do we sometimes want who we can't have?
8. Is it true that it's better to have loved and lost than never to have loved at all?
9. Is it true that while the cat's away the mice will play?
10. Who most often wins in a battle of the sexes?
11. When will you allow your child to start dating?
12. Would you want your child to date someone like you?

12

PUBLIC SPEAKING

"Why don't we like to speak in front of a crowd?"

I'm sure it was inevitable that I added this question to the mix, but surprisingly, I really wasn't all that interested in its response during those first few years. For some reason, I just felt like it was cheap to ask a question about speaking during a speaking exercise. Maybe I just wasn't that meta yet.

When I was in second grade, I volunteered to read at the annual Talent Show. Clearly, I misunderstood what a talent show was supposed to highlight because reading isn't really a talent, per se. At that age, however, no teacher was going to deny a volunteer request, so reading was my talent. I chose to read Shel Silverstein's "Sick" from his seminal work, *Where the Sidewalk Ends*. At the time, I was obsessed with Silverstein's work, both written and drawn, and I couldn't get my hands on enough of his books to read. I'd like to think he was a very early inspiration when I launched my writing career during the following year, specializing in stories of time travel and fantasy. Sadly, my work was not received well by critics, but my teachers loved it.

Dressed in a gray suit with a maroon tie, I delivered the poem with grace and humor; at least, that's what my parents told me. I remember really gearing up for those final three lines: *"What? What's that? What's that you say?/You say today is...Saturday?/G'bye, I'm going out to play!"* as if I were delivering my acceptance speech after being named Poet Laureate. Next, I remember the applause, which drowned out the smattering of "awwwwws," to which no parent is immune. Lastly, I remember trying desperately to squelch the smile as it curled because I knew, in that moment, that I loved to be in front of a crowd.

Four years later, I was selected to be part of a triumvirate of 6th-grade graduation speakers, each of whom would address the class's past, present, and future. I had the enviable task of discussing our collective future, one I still enjoy with several grammar school friends.

Six years later, I volunteered, again, to speak during our high school's Baccalaureate ceremony, this time focusing on the indelible closeness of our class, on our mutual love for grunge music and Natural Lite, and on our long-since unfulfilled promise to remain that close forever. I even sneaked in a few shout-outs to teachers who helped me get to that podium.

I guess my point is I wasn't really interested in this prompt because it didn't apply to me. So much of my focus for every question I created was on how I had lived or was curious about how kids had lived their answers. To ask kids to address their aversion to public speaking seemed, frankly, like a waste of time. It took years of using the activity and seeing the often universal combination of sweat, hives, and eye contact refusal to understand that this was something about which we *should* be talking. Ultimately, I decided that if I was going to ask kids to talk about the often unspoken, I needed to ask about the spoken as well.

When I began to use the question regularly, that is, when it was selected, I noticed, somewhat unremarkably, that answers followed the same basic pattern:

Kid A: Ugh, I don't know. I don't like this question.

Kid B: Because it's, like, you know, hard.

Kid C: No one does, man. Everyone is, like, looking at you.

Essentially, kids rarely referenced their own idiosyncrasies, concerns about content or context, or even their grades. It was invariably the reaction of their peers that caused so much anxiety. Of course, anxiety manifests itself in a number of ways. Some kids giggle uncontrollably, some kids turn disturbing shades of red, and some kids sit in incredibly awkward silence while both cursing my very name and praying that they will be dismissed back to their seats. Still, the common denominator in almost all my kids' reactions to this question was fear of judgment.

"At the time, I was afraid of it [the Hot Seat]. My response was rather simple, 'I am afraid of being judged because there is always going to be someone out there in the audience who does not agree with whatever I am saying,'" reflected Cassie M., the middle of three siblings, all of whom I taught. A bright, quiet senior in my honors class, Cassie sat right in the middle of the room, and she struck me as the kind of girl who always had plenty on her mind, but that little of it made it to our ears.

I'm always amazed at how much I learn about my kids, both because of the Hot Seat and because of how our post-graduation relationship, albeit often as online friends or followers, changes. Cassie belied her self-confidence as a student in my class, something foreign to us both now as she went to become an elementary school teacher and because Cassie has the kind of personality to which people gravitate. Yet, here she was, admitting that she could not stomach the idea of people disagreeing with her.

"No one laughed at me, and quite a few people agreed with me, but there was one person who did not fear being judged. Instead [he admitted that] having twenty people staring at him while talking [was his fear]. And that proved my point because someone disagreed with me. They did not try to argue with me, but instead informed me that everyone's fear may not be the same. I still believe what I said, years later, but I can't stop people from having opinions, and I definitely can't force everyone to think like me."

Here's where Cassie, and so many students like her, and I are philosophically aligned. People like us spend so much time in our own heads, a place often as comfortable as it is lonely, in fear of having someone disagree with us. When she and I spoke about this, I used the following example: I cannot accept that people still smoke. I don't get it, and I never will. Still, and maybe this is something Cassie taught me, my strong opinion against smoking shouldn't preclude me from speaking out against it any more than Cassie's initial aversion to public speaking should deter her from doing so. If anything, convincing ourselves that what is rattling inside our heads needs to come out, regardless of the reaction it may cause, is paramount to success in the Hot Seat and in life.

Argument, debate, and discussion are so often combined, confused, and bastardized that we sometimes succumb to apathy as an antidote. We have to teach our kids to develop their own opinions, to seek out opportunities and platforms in which to voice them, to prepare for opposition and to address it with aplomb. It is too easy to just dismiss voices other than our own, especially in an online world in which many of our voices are seen rather than heard. Instead, we have to empower our kids to use their voices, their way. The only way to do that, as I said during the introduction, is to listen.

————

Kyra M.'s experience is not unlike Cassie's; however, her reaction to the Hot Seat involves more layers, more backstory. I remember Kyra and her time in the chair well, and reconnecting with her about her experience was incredibly powerful.

Unlike Cassie, Kyra came to English IV (CP) from an admittedly dysfunctional home, punctuated by her mother's alcoholism. She sat in the center of the room, directly in front of my podium, though often hidden by long, dark hair, which would cover her face. At the beginning of the year, as is the case every year, kids are often timid as we try to feel each other out. They had the benefit of hearing about my class and style from friends and siblings; on the other hand, I often had no idea who these kids were or what they were bringing to my room every day. I could tell Kyra was guarded, sort of closed off and speculative in a way that suggested her discomfort. It wasn't until our more recent conversations that I learned much of that early persona could be attributed to her already growing fear of the Hot Seat.

"[Before entering your class] I had heard about a classmate I went to middle school with. He had gone up on the Hot Seat and spoke of his family issues. We had very similar family situations and when we were in middle school together there was not one person who didn't know about our families. When I heard my classmates talking about what he had talked about, many of them were surprised; they had no idea."

Here we see the root of so much public speaking angst. On one hand, Kyra was adamant that "everyone knew about my family." However, on the other hand, she admitted to her own surprise that so many people with whom she had grown up had no idea about her family. In essence, she had created a scenario in which she was the daughter of an alcoholic whom everyone knew, so she couldn't possibly earn the respect or admiration of her peers, especially not through a venue like the Hot Seat.

The problem with that scenario is that it was all in her head.

As a result, Kyra would often contort herself into pretzelian positions and refuse to make eye contact with me during the Hot Seat in early 2009. In her mind, exposing herself to her peers after years of what she perceived as sideways glances and hushed judgments, was something she just couldn't do.

"I spent my entire life fighting any and every moment I would have to stand in front of my class and speak. Even in middle school, [in front of] a group of people that I knew very well, I could not muster up the courage to speak in front of them. In sixth grade we had public speaking all year, and I had managed to only give one speech (don't ask me how I passed). When Hot Seat was explained to the class, I panicked! I absolutely could not do this, but when I was called up and sat in the seat I felt nothing but calm. I was asked my question and answered it, and after getting up, I could not wait to do it again.

"I'm still not exactly sure what made me feel that calm, but it was the same feeling every time. I couldn't wait to share my thoughts and feelings on any number of things. To this day, that was the only time I felt completely at ease speaking to a group."

Immediately, I wondered, *why*? What happened between the anxiety of waiting to take a turn and the very short walk back to her desk after her answer that changed everything for Kyra?

"I believe my fear of public speaking came from a very intense self-esteem and self-confidence problem. I was a very awkward child/pre-teen and I grew up in a small town where everyone knew the details of my life. I think that the thought of standing in front of my peers, even to discuss how to bake a cake, felt like all they were thinking were hurtful things about me and my family or how awkward my appearance was. That feeling never left me.

"I went into my senior year excited and fearful all at the same time. I knew that my time left in high school was very short and that was hard for me. After watching classmates before me get up and answer their questions, I felt a little more at ease until my turn came. I shook all the way up the chair, and as soon as I sat down, I could never understand it, but I felt the most ease I ever felt in front of a class. I was given my question and as soon as I started to give my answer I looked up in front of my class and realized that I was actually being listened to. It didn't feel like I was being judged; it felt like I was finally being heard.

"That was the best I had felt in school in a long time. I believe what helped me overcome that fear for the Hot Seat was the content and the situation. I think the questions being asked felt like someone cared about our (my) opinions on adult and controversial topics. With these questions and the little time we had left, my classmates could understand a small part of me."

The first thing you may notice is that she doesn't even address what her original question or answer were. Much like what people *may have thought* about her mom or *may have thought* about Kyra's appearance, it really didn't matter. What mattered is that for what was likely the first time, someone listened to Kyra. Instead of being stuck in her own head, a place we already discussed as being very confining, she allowed herself to speak up.

For herself.

From that moment on, I could always count on Kyra for discussion-driving questions. She seemed to have a perpetually raised hand, and whether she knew it or not, she no longer sat contorted in her desk. And she most certainly made eye contact. All the time.

What I learned from Cassie and Kyra is not that the Hot Seat created students in its image. Rather, students made the Hot Seat what they needed it to be.

For some, it became a confessional.

For others, it became a pulpit.

For still others, it became a mirror.

For Cassie and Kyra, it became a window.

———

Class Reunion with John S. (Class of 2011)

Public speaking sucks. It's generally on a topic that is so boring it can make the teacher fall asleep, not to mention the other twenty classmates. The standard public speaking assignment is nerve-racking, but there is always the solace that no one is paying attention because the presenter does not even care about the topic he or she is speaking about.

The Hot Seat served as an enjoyable way to get over the fear of talking in front of a group of people and was effective because it always sparked a topic worth hearing about that kept the audience intrigued, and the presenter engaged in thinking, rather than worrying about flipping through the heavily-recited note cards, and hoping you hit your mark for the permitted time limit.

The Hot Seat certainly foreshadowed the same feelings of freshman year of college, by getting every individual out of their comfort zone and feeling the same way as the person next to you. The Hot Seat was able to make everyone feel the same nervous energy before going in front of a class that would surely be paying attention. High school can be a place where many people feel very vulnerable, and public speaking makes anyone that much more susceptible to criticism from peers. It definitely prepared me for the many future public speaking assignments in college and in my professional career in politics.

13

GRADING THE HOT SEAT

Like I mentioned earlier, you'd be surprised at how infrequently I heard: *What did I get?*

Despite the fact that we live in a world in which we are constantly assessing kids, the scores kids earned as part of the activity rarely seemed to matter. While it's true that in its earliest incarnation, the activity was basically a free "A" to those who participated (call it guerilla marketing), I never agonized over what a student earned, never forced myself to give verbal or tacit validation of any particular answer, and never used the activity as a bargaining chip, threat, or promise. Because of its immediate success during that first year, grades became an afterthought.

Although I'm convinced I could have used the activity weekly and never assigned a grade, I caved to perceived administrative pressure to provide a score in my gradebook. As a young teacher trying something for the first time, I really couldn't risk the kind of backlash that would accompany what some would consider a weekly conversation about life if I couldn't justify its educational value through a score from 0-100. Somehow, doing so cheapened the experience for me, but sometimes, we just have to concede.

During the first several years, the scoring was based on very subjective criteria focused on creating a safe environment in which to answer difficult questions meaningfully.

- Did you answer the question with honesty and maturity?
- Did you provide relevant, experiential examples from your life to support your answer?
- Did you rely on me to walk you through the answer?

As you can see, such criteria lends itself to success with the understanding that this is a collective activity in which we all participate, myself included, and that I'm much more interested in *what you say* rather than *how you say it.*

Eventually, the activity became something students looked forward to before they even got to my class. Before long, I saw an opportunity to brand the activity. I shared the activity with colleagues in my building and beyond. I used it with a group of teachers who were part of a county professional development consortium. I started to add questions whenever they occurred to me and to remove questions that no longer held any relevance or just weren't very thought-provoking. Finally, while coaching baseball one day, I decided it was time to tweak how I scored the activity.

I was going to use my pitch counter.

Because this bizarre, and slightly sadistic, epiphany came to me late in the spring semester, I had the summer to focus on how I was going to change the expectations and scoring for use with students the following year. Immediately, I recognized that I didn't want to introduce the pitch counter to strike fear and to make an already nauseating activity for some an even more imposing proposition. I would have to build toward the use of the "clicker."

First, I decided the activity no longer worked as a standalone. Because, invariably, kids had heard about the activity as under-classmen, I no longer had to sell each class on its purpose or efficacy. Their friends and siblings had already done my marketing. Instead, I would dangle the Hot Seat as the culmination of a very brief, but very fast-paced crash course on effective public speaking. Whether it was based on my age or my years of listening to kids speaking in class or a combination of the two, I became acutely aware of some of the more nuanced similarities among teenage speech patterns: vocal fry, fillers, fidgeting, and eye contact. While I was wholly aware of these facets of public speaking as an adult and with reference to my own speech patterns and foibles (I speak incredibly fast and often jumble words together), I never really considered that which makes teenage public speaking distinctly, well, teenage.

But here I had this established platform for improving the public speaking acumen of all my students, and I wasn't taking full advantage. Something needed to change.

I began to scour YouTube for both excellent and cringeworthy public speaking examples. Chief among them were excerpts from speeches by Presidents Obama and Kennedy (excellent) and now infamous clips like "Boom Goes the Dynamite" and Miss South Carolina, Lauren Caitlin Upton, whose Miss Teen USA 2007 pageant answer to a question about maps made her a most unfortunate internet sensation.

Next, I created a very basic presentation on that which makes for a quality public speaking experience, the details of which I won't bore you with here. Suffice it to say, I provided my students with a foundation on which to build their own public speaking brand. We talked about inflection, largely through media personalities; the pregnant pause, an effective alternative to fillers like um, nahmeen (nee: you know what I mean?); eye contact tricks like looking directly over the heads of the audience and focusing on the back wall; posture (I don't know what to do with my hands!); and resisting the urge to fidget, sway, twirl hair, crack knuckles, etc. We even provided ourselves with the ultimate stall for more time, *"That's a great question; let me think about it."* Before long, we even began to throw out our gum *before* taking our turn in the Hot Seat.

When my students were equipped with a foundation for effective public speaking, it was time to hold them accountable. Because the original intention of the activity was to engage in an intimate, meaningful discussion, I always ran the activity as a two-way conversation. Although I had considered opening up the discussion while the student was still in the Hot Seat, I ultimately thought better of it for fear of the unknown. I didn't want anyone to feel like he was in front of a firing squad at the mercy of his peers; instead, I would handle the follow-up discussion, and if audience members wanted to chime in, they could do so on my terms.

Years of experience and a bit of naivete caused me to change my mind. As I reflected on the totality of the activity, I realized I was only tapping into 1/20ish of the students in the class during any given answer. So what if someone decided to go off the rails and ask a follow up that was inappropriate or immature? I would handle that disruption like I would any other. So, from that point on, I committed to opening up the activity to more of a town hall meeting style.

After a student was finished with a question, the audience was free to ask follow-up questions. At first, I promised the participant that she was "off the clock" and that whatever she said after I finished my feedback was "free of charge." However, after about a month-long trial period that following September, I realized that kids should be able to speak in this kind of forum regardless of who is asking the questions. The same rules would apply: Answer fully and with honesty, avoid common public speaking pitfalls, and use whatever examples from your own experience that you can muster.

Opening up the discussion had an immediate and transcendent effect. Because students realized they were going to be allowed to ask follow up questions, they listened more intently than they did in the past. Moreover, audience members allowed their wheels to turn out loud when they heard a question they loved or an answer they wanted to debate. One caveat to any question was that once it was asked, it was off the list. Because of this, kids were often disappointed that they weren't able to answer a question they wished they had, so now anyone could answer any question, any time. Additionally, the student in the chair no longer had the benefit of my follow up questions, which are always meant to foster further discussion, to support a struggling answerer, or to continue an answer about which I was genuinely interested. So, every question applied to every student, all the time.

Still further, I started to invite the audience to provide feedback to each speaker. This was a tenuous line to walk at first. Again, there is just no accounting for petty grudges, general meanness, or reprisal for a formerly broken heart, but I just couldn't pass up the opportunity for students to talk to each other *about* each other. After any given answer, I would open up the discussion by asking the same thing, *"What did you see? What did you hear?"* This was vague enough to allow both celebrations and criticisms. It also forced kids to create an adult-based headspace through which they could be assertive and nurturing. Comments almost invariably fell into two categories: Effusive praise on a job well done or a reference to how many mistakes the speaker made.

Now, back to the pitch counter.

I thought about how I could score kids with more fidelity than I had in the past, and I wanted to hold them accountable for that which we covered in class. The way I saw it, there wasn't enough pressure to succeed while in the Hot Seat, so I was concerned that the activity was devolving into a dog-and-pony show for some of my less motivated kids. While it may seem like a cruel and unusual practice to infuse *more pressure* into the activity, my kids needed to be aware that when they spoke in public beyond my room, I wouldn't be there to support them.

So, I started to "click" them.

Students were told that for every fundamental mistake they made based on the introductory lessons I gave, they would receive one click on the pitch counter.

10 "ummmms" = 10 clicks.

Poor posture = 1 click.

1,245 "likes" = 1,245 clicks.

Each click represented one point off the final grade for speaking acumen. Then, they would receive a score based on what they said. In this way, they could recover from a poorly spoken answer by providing a meaningful answer. Then, the two numbers would average out, and, again, kids tended to do really well.

Still, the clicker became a bit of a poltergeist in the room.

Everyone knew it was there, hidden neatly under my desk, but no one knew how many times it was clicking unless they listened very hard. But no one did because they were too busy listening to the answer coming from The Hot Seat.

Ultimately, the changes I made to scoring the activity did little to move the needle on the impact of any answer. Simply, kids just didn't care about the grade, and that was kind of the point. If given a choice, my kids were more likely to ask to go again than to ask how I scored them. In fact, in all my conversations with former students over the years, exactly *one* has referred to his grade (you'll meet him at the end of the chapter). I would argue that some even forgot that a score was part of the Hot Seat.

Whether the powers that be want to admit it or not, so much of what happens in our classrooms doesn't include a rubric, can't be standardized, and never makes it into a gradebook. Rather, the most meaningful and transcendent part of our field is experiential and relational.

Neither of which should be graded.

———

Class Reunion Pat B. (Class of 2001):

So I don't remember the exact question or what led me to this answer, but I was somehow talking about having the motivation to come back to our HS reunion incredibly successful and pull up in some expensive car (maybe a Lamborghini?). Kulak said something to the effect of, "and why do you want to do that?" and I said "I dunno, just to be a dick I guess," and he said in a hilarious and totally deadpan way that still sticks with me, "you can't say dick on the Hot Seat." Then he gave me a B, and I believe I was the only person to not get an A on the assignment. Side note: my answer embarrasses me greatly because I've spent enough time around rich people now to know that material possessions are in no way indicative of a person's success. I hate everything about my answer - the pettiness, the weird motivation of flexing on my old classmates...everything about the answer was awful. Except for the cursing. I actually stand by that.

Unfortunately, I have a *terrible* memory. It's the thing I'd most like to change about myself. I'm not hyperbolizing when I say I remember three individual moments from classes in high school, and the Hot Seat is one of them. It was so much more impactful than any other lesson could've been. And for me personally, it was a unique vehicle to express myself. I was comfortable speaking publicly but also something of an introvert, but I immediately felt at home on the Hot Seat and enjoyed expressing my thoughts to a captive audience. I also liked getting some laughs.

Three years after the Hot Seat I started doing stand-up, and twenty years after that I'm living in LA and writing comedy professionally. Crazy as it sounds, I think the Hot Seat was my first real exposure to public speaking and probably eased the transition into trying standup.

CONCLUSION

As I was wrapping up my final edits, I got this instant message on Facebook:

> Hey Brian, I hope all is well! I had a question for you. I am teaching public speaking and I wanted to add Hot Seat to the curriculum like we did when I had you. Any shot somewhere in your collection of educational tools, you have a bunch of topics for the Hot Seat? Thanks so much, hope you're doing well brother!

It was from Joe W., class of 2001.

So a student I taught 24 years ago reached out about the activity I was writing about that started 24 years ago. Let that sink in. We met for coffee shortly thereafter, and I gave him everything I had.

The world and its educational landscape during which I started teaching is barely recognizable today. Absent smartphones and watches, of influencers and social media, we were still using soon-to-be-archaic overhead projectors and textbooks. Our weekly lesson plans were written by hand, our instruction was devoid of flashy multimedia, and our conversations with each other were face-to-face. And while we could argue that our careers were much harder because we didn't have all the bells and whistles of today's teaching crop, we could also argue that such made us better because we had to rely on ourselves. And on each other.

Nostalgia has a funny way of being in the eye of the beholder.

Despite all that we might hearken back to with a shudder or a smile, there is at least one immutable fact about education: We are in the "business" of people. We are in loco parentis, and we are forward facing. We are on stage, and we are behind the scenes. We are confidants, and we are champions. We are beloved, and we are beleaguered.

We are always in the Hot Seat.

And we chose this profession because we love kids. Your kids.

For parents, The Hot Seat proves how crucial it is to keep talking to your kids, even when it seems like that's the last thing they want to do.

For aspiring and current educators, The Hot Seat provides a ready-to-use activity that can be re-imagined to fit the needs of their kids.

For me, the Hot Seat had little to do with its questions and answers and everything to do with the students sitting in it.

So talk to your kids.

Talk to them about the mundane and about the magnificent.

Talk to them about their now and about their later.

Talk to them about the light and about the dark.

Talk to them when they can't talk to their parents.

Talk to them *so they can* talk to their parents.

Because in the end, the "temperature" of the seat doesn't matter.

What matters is that we owe it to our kids to provide the seat.

THE QUESTIONS

As promised, this is the final list of questions I used before I left the classroom in 2014. Its iterations and motivations changed right alongside with me as I wrote them. But any good list comes from within, is fluid, and is personal. Still, these can serve as a foundation on which to build your own, so have at it!

1. Of what have you been deprived?
2. Describe yourself or your family in one word. Explain.
3. Are you ready for what lies after graduation?
4. Are you marriage material?
5. Knowing yourself, what is the one thing in life which you know you can't handle?
6. Outside of a parent, choose the one person who has helped you become who you are.
7. Do you find yourself to be more anxious or relaxed?
8. How would you describe your childhood?
9. Do you typically finish what you start?
10. When was the last time you cried and was it worth it?
11. What is your life missing right now?
12. What is your worst quality?
13. When you graduate, do you see yourself coming back here to live or never coming back at all?
14. What are you too old for right now? Not old enough?
15. About what do you most worry?
16. If you were asked to create and direct a reality series about high school, how would you portray this culture? How would you cast, what would you have to include, what would you leave out?
17. Do you judge others by higher or lower standards than you judge yourself?
18. You are asked to choose between a soulmate and no close friends or several close friends and no soulmate. Which would you choose and why?

19. How many of your friendships have lasted throughout high school and what does that say about such friendships?

20. What has been the biggest disappointment in your life so far? How do you think you handled it?

21. Do you consider yourself a better talker or listener?

22. If I guaranteed you an honest response to any question, what would you ask and of whom?

23. Is it more difficult/frightening to look ahead or look back?

24. Recall your first day as a student (in high school) and describe that feeling or walk us through the day. Now put yourself in your first college class. Do you think the feeling will be the same?

25. What is one of the biggest problems facing a person your age and/or gender right now?

26. When you leave high school, how do you think you'll be remembered? How should you be remembered?

27. Are you good with money?

28. If you weren't you, would you be friends with you?

29. Is there a difference between being alone and being lonely?

30. Is it easier for a good kid to go bad or a bad kid to go good?

31. Is there any difference between a reason and an excuse?

32. How important are/were grandparents in your life?

33. Are you a good manipulator?

34. Is there a difference between accepting and settling?

35. Give me a good example of an exception to the rule.

36. How important is being popular?

37. What is the biggest decision you've had to make so far?

38. At what age do you think it's possible to fall in love?

39. Should there be an age requirement for dating?

40. What single event, conversation, or decision has most influenced you so far?

41. If you could go back in time and change something, what would it be?

42. If you could live in someone else's shoes, whose would they be and how long would you stay?

43. What do you most cherish?

44. If you knew you were going to die, what would you want to have accomplished?

45. Would you want to know how and when you were to die?

46. Do nice guys finish last?

47. Can one person really make a difference?

48. Do you believe in fate?

49. What is your opinion of the expression, "If it feels good do it?"

50. What happens after we die?

51. What have you learned about yourself in the past two years?

52. To whom do you most look up and why?

53. Do you think people who go out of their way to be different are really the same as people who go out of their way to be the same?
54. What do you expect from a normal week at college?
55. What are you most afraid of—beyond the conventional spiders, the dark, etc.
56. Does peer pressure still exist?
57. Is the unknown more terrifying or exhilarating?
58. Why do people consciously do harm to themselves?
59. How strong are your friendships?
60. Who is a "bigger" person, the one who apologizes or the one who accepts?
61. What is the true measure of a "good" person?
62. Is most betrayal planned or accidental?
63. What is more exciting: anticipation or realization?
64. Is it really possible for any of us to change?
65. What is annoying?
66. Why do we often want who we can't have?
67. Is it true that it's better to have loved and lost than never to have loved at all?
68. Why do we lie?
69. Why do people deem it necessary to have a "best" friend?
70. What is the most embarrassing thing that's ever happened to you?
71. What is petty to you?
72. What is comforting?
73. What does everyone deserve?

74. Why do we gossip?
75. All things considered, what constitutes a good weekend?
76. Is it true that while the cat's away the mice will play?
77. Who most often wins in a battle of the sexes?
78. To what do you most look forward?
79. What do you think of the line, "There's nothing worse in life than being ordinary?"
80. What is the most important thing in your life right now?
81. What is your personal meaning of life?
82. How important is it for you to "find someone?"
83. Should there be an age for adulthood?
84. Is it better to be honest and hurt someone or lie and protect him/her?
85. Do you consider yourself a hypocrite?
86. Is it more important to love or to be loved?
87. What makes you laugh?
88. When will you allow your child to start dating?
89. Are you capable of murder?
90. If you were reincarnated, what would you come back as?
91. What could the world do without?
92. Why?
93. Describe yourself at age 7.
94. What is one lesson you have been taught throughout your life that you will always remember?

95. Tell one of the funniest things that you've witnessed or experienced.

96. Describe what you want your children to be like? Would you like them to be like yourself or totally different?

97. If your parents split, with whom would you live or how did you come to live with the parent you do?

98. Who means more to you: mom or dad?

99. What do you think your parents were like at your age?

100. Do you think that some people are afraid to succeed in life?

101. If you had memory issues and could pick one thing to remember/forget what or who would it be?

102. What's your favorite place in the world and why?

103. What is your favorite high school memory and why?

104. How much do you really pay attention—in life, in class, in relationships?

105. What would the 18 year old you say to the 8 year old you?

106. How many phases have you gone through in your life?

107. Are you more likely to cover for someone or have someone cover for you?

108. Do you want your kids to end up following the same path as you?

109. How would you define your own life?

110. Is there anything in your life for which you feel you should have been rewarded/recognized but haven't been?

111. How much of your life has seams (as in gaps)/seems (as in indefinites)?

112. Would you want your child to date someone like you?

113. How much of what you have has been earned?

114. Discuss why you think some people are just mean.

115. If given a choice, would you rather endure emotional or physical pain? Why?

116. Are you more aware of your insides or your outsides?

117. Do you think you'll have a better life than your parents?

118. Who would you want to eulogize you and what would you want that person to say?

Time to create your own!

Many chairs were used over the years, but thanks to Siobhan Sullivan, class of 2009, there is only one Hot Seat.

ABOUT THE AUTHOR

Brian Kulak is in his 26th year in education. For the first fifteen, he taught English and journalism at his alma mater in New Jersey. Working almost exclusively with seniors, Brian was committed to making connections with his students, so they could make connections with their world. He has also served as chief academic officer and is currently a K-5 principal in New Jersey.

In 2019, Brian published his first book, *Level Up Leadership: Advance Your EduGame*. Using the evolution of the gaming industry, the book blends gaming nostalgia, educational philosophy, and practical leadership strategies.

His blog, briankulak.net, combines shared educational experience with self-effacing humor, pop culture, and storytelling, and challenges readers to view themselves and their leadership differently.

His work has been featured on Edutopia, in *Educational Viewpoints*, and in *Stories in EDU*. Brian has also presented on teaching, learning, and leadership at conferences such as NJAMLE and NCTE/CEL.

Brian is a baseball fanatic, a Pearl Jam aficionado, and a devoted family man. He lives in New Jersey with his two children and their dog.

BIBLIOGRAPHY

Albom, Mitch. *Tuesdays With Morrie*. Doubleday, 1997.

Boy Meets World. Created by Michael Jacobs, and April Kelly, ABC, 1993.

Chbosky, Stephen. *The Perks of Being a Wallflower*. MTV Book/Pocket Books, 1999.

Golding, William. Lord of the Flies . Faber and Faber, 1954.

Head of the Class. Created by Michael Elias, and Richard Eustis, ABC, 1986.

Hershon, Joanna. *Swimming*. Ballantine Books, 2002.

O'Dell, Tawni. *Back Roads*. New American Library, 2004.

Perrotta, Tom. *Joe College*. St. Martin's Griffin, 2006.

Salinger, JD. *The Catcher In The Rye*. Little, Brown, and Company, 1951.

Shakespeare, William. *Macbeth*. 1606.

Shakespeare, William. *Romeo and Juliet*. 1597.

Silverstein, Shel. *Where the Sidewalk Ends*. Harper and Row, 1974.

Waters, Mark, director. *Mean Girls*. Paramount Pictures, 2004.

Weir, Peter, director. *Dead Poets Society*. Touchstone Pictures, 1989.

EDUMATCH